A.

Resources
and
Population

Resources
and Population

Proceedings of the Ninth Annual
Symposium of the Eugenics Society
London 1972

Edited by
BERNARD BENJAMIN
Civil Service College,
London

PETER R. COX
Government Actuary's Department,
London

JOHN PEEL
Teesside Polytechnic,
Middlesbrough, Teesside

1973

Academic Press · London · New York
A subsidiary of Harcourt Brace Jovanovich, Publishers

ACADEMIC PRESS INC. (LONDON) LTD.
24/28 Oval Road,
London, NW1

United States Edition published by
ACADEMIC PRESS INC.
111 Fifth Avenue
New York, New York 10003

Library of Congress Catalog Card Number: 73-1471
ISBN: 0-12-088 350-3

PRINTED IN GREAT BRITAIN BY
Lonsdale Universal Printing Ltd., Larkhall, Bath, Somerset

Contributors

F. J. C. Amos, City Planning Department, Wilberforce House,
25 The Strand, Liverpool, England

M. D. I. Chisholm, Department of Geography, University of Bristol,
England

John I. Clarke, Department of Geography, University of Durham,
England

Bleddyn Davies, Department of Social Administration,
London School of Economics, England

John Davoll, The Conservation Society, 34 Bridge Street,
Walton-on-Thames, Surrey, England

C. I. K. Forster, 29a Ashley Gardens, London, England

David Hall, Town and Country Planning Association,
17 Carlton House Terrace, London, England

Margaret Haswell, Queen Elizabeth House, Oxford, England

T. H. Hollingsworth, Department of Social and Economic Research,
University of Glasgow, Scotland

F. W. Hutber, Department of Trade and Industry, London, England

J. H. Lawton, Department of Biology, University of York, England

J. E. Meade, Christ's College, Cambridge, England

B. Rydz, Water Resources Board, Reading Bridge House,
Reading, Berkshire, England

P. V. Sukhatme, Gokhale Institute of Politics and Economics,
Poona, India

Preface

In arranging the Symposium of which this book is the record, we had in mind the need both for a comprehensive review of the problem and for some freshness of approach to a well-known topic. Moreover, those aspects which received attention in *Population and Pollution*, the allied subject of the Society's preceding Symposium, did not in general require further treatment after so short an interval. Indeed, the book is part of a continuing series of publications each one of which stands on its own but also is related with some care to the contents of the others.

The task of the Editors was made the easier because of the willingness of those who were asked to participate both to deliver their talks lucidly and to produce manageable scripts.

The Editors express their grateful thanks to Miss F. Schenk for her assistance in the organization of the Symposium and of the editorial work connected with the preparation of this volume.

On behalf of the Eugenics Society
BERNARD BENJAMIN
PETER R. COX
JOHN PEEL

JANUARY 1973

Contents

General Introduction:

From Domesday to Doomsday?

MICHAEL CHISHOLM

Department of Geography, University of Bristol, England

When scientists take umbrage and call into question each other's integrity, the layman may be forgiven for supposing that something is amiss. Thus, the spectacle of many eminent scientists issuing "A blueprint for survival" in *The Ecologist* (1972), and the violent reactions of Mr John Maddox (1972), editor of *Nature,* is at once entertaining and disturbing. An equally virulent reaction against prophecies of impending ecological doom was elicited from the economist, Professor W. Beckerman (1972), in his inaugural lecture. When optimist confronts pessimist, the one will proclaim the bottle to be still half full and the other that it is already half empty. Both are right and yet the implications of both positions are worlds apart.

I do not intend to engage in a bout of academic fisticuffs but rather to highlight what I think are some of the essential issues concerning man's use of the natural environment and what, if anything, should be done to curb the consumption of resources and limit the dispersal of harmful materials into the atmosphere, waters and soil. I personally do not subscribe to the view that the end of man, indeed of the world, is just around the corner. The latter-day pessimists rationalize their fears in material terms, whereas previous generations feared the wrath of God. Nor do I believe, with Dr Pangloss, that all will be for the best in the best of all possible worlds—or even this imperfect world. The truth lies between these extremes and consists of two fundamental propositions.

1. We, as a nation, and the world as a whole, are faced with novel problems in relation to the environment. Furthermore, we do not know the full nature and significance of these problems.
2. Despite the extraordinary advances made in recent years in devising ways to control our collective actions (birth control programmes in India and elsewhere, smoke abatement laws and subsidies for railway systems both in Britain and elsewhere, etc), the whole art of social management is in its infancy—is indeed fiercely rejected by many of the younger generation.

The novel problems are presented by two incontrovertible facts concerning the recent history of mankind: the sustained rapid growth of population during the past 200 years; the rapid increase in personal consumption in some countries and growing technological sophistication that has been part-and-parcel of economic growth. The problems themselves can be grouped under three headings.

1. Will food supplies be adequate to nourish the millions of prospective inhabitants of the world?
2. Will there be an adequate supply of the non-renewable, and some renewable, resources (e.g. iron, oil, aluminium and whales) to sustain the modern industrial society of the developed world and allow its replication in the developing Third World?
3. Can the pollution of the environment be controlled so as to avoid permanent damage to the world's ecological balance?

One reason for the high state of feelings on these problems is the failure of protagonists to disaggregate the issues. Furthermore, propositions valid in one context have been transferred to other situations, where their relevance is questionable.

Perhaps I may illustrate the nature of this confusion by reference to Beckerman's onslaught on the Doomsday men. On the question of non-renewable resources, he concludes:

> As for raw materials becoming exhausted, it is most unlikely that this will cause any dislocation.

This conclusion is probably correct and is based on two elementary propositions. First, the exhaustion of resources would not occur overnight. Second, increasing scarcity implies higher prices and the search for economies in use, for substitutes and methods of re-use. In other words, the market economy will look after the problems as they arise. However, it is not tenable to go on to say that:

> As for pollution, this is really no problem at all as far as devising the correct solution is concerned.

Elsewhere, Beckerman blandly says:

> Elementary economics tells us that the reason why there is a pollution problem is that the environment does not carry a price representing its correct social scarcity value.

If it is such a simple matter to determine social scarcity value, I wonder why the Roskill Commission ran into such fierce criticism in its attempt to measure social costs and benefits in the choice of London's third airport? Or, in the same vein, can we really conceive of an administrative machinery that would allow the citizens of Norway to levy a tax at the "correct" rate on British users of petroleum products for the damage caused by the sulphuric acid that—literally—rains from the Norwegian sky? And how much harder it would be to envisage such arrangements where the cash economy is still grossly under-developed, where by definition the market economy is very imperfect. Furthermore, when the practicality of regulating pollution by charging the polluters is examined at some length in the Minority Report in the recent annual report of the Royal Commission on Environmental Pollution (1972), the principle that is advocated differs substantially from the notion of setting a social price on the environment. It becomes much more like a charge representing the cost of treating the pollutant to reduce pollution to some arbitrarily "acceptable" level—which begs most of the real questions.

At this point, two general comments are relevant. To regard the man/ecology set of problems as a matter of resource allocation implies that the paraphernalia of economic analysis is applicable. Yet fundamental to this mode of analysis is the discounting of future costs and benefits at some rate of interest At any reasonable interest rate, the future that is more than 20 years away has very little impact on current values. And yet many of the environmental concerns arise from issues that clearly relate to time periods far in excess of 20 years. I would personally argue that, for this reason alone, the armoury of techniques for resource allocation turns out to be an empty citadel. It follows that a whole variety of criteria is likely to be relevant in making decisions about resources on space-ship Earth, that these may be in conflict and that, therefore, in the last resort subjective judgement is necessary.

The second general comment is that despite the vast amount of research that has been accomplished over the last century or two, we remain woefully ignorant concerning the magnitude and geographical extent of changes in ecological systems. Most particularly, we know little about the thresholds for *irreversible* changes of an adverse kind; for example, whether the accumulation of carbon dioxide in the atmosphere could produce a "glasshouse" effect that could not then be remedied and, if so, at what level of concentration of CO_2?

So far, my remarks have been pitched at a general level, in an attempt to establish terms of reference within which sensible discussion can proceed. I want briefly to continue in the same vein and then turn to some practical issues on which action can and should be taken. In our everyday lives, we are accustomed to making choices. The essential characteristic of such choices is the trading of one possible course of action against another. To do this, we have certain goals, aspirations or needs and are constrained by factors like income, time available, our health, etc. We try to identify the choices that realistically are available to us and evaluate them in terms of our individual preferences. In so doing, we engage in a complicated calculus in which the criteria are measured in very disparate terms—from pounds and pence to aesthetic satisfaction.

We are also accustomed to the concept of multiple goals in the context of town and country planning. The history of planning is, in fact, particularly interesting, as it demonstrates an important issue relevant to the wider environmental controversy. The early days of planning consisted very largely of the setting of certain arbitrary standards for things like housing density, provision of open space and distance between home and school. Many of these standards, as embodied in the Parker Morris house specifications for example, have antecedents in the Public Health Acts of the nineteenth century. These standards were set on the basis of very limited information about the real effects of the various provisions on human health and happiness and have in fact been called in question in recent years.

The key point that I am trying to make is two-fold. In the first place, all matters concerned with the natural environment are ones in which there are multiple criteria and multiple interests. In principle, therefore, it is unlikely that there can be a single "right" answer. As a corollary, it is proper that individuals and groups, and indeed nations, shall express their own views on what should or should not be done. Collective decisions depend on viewpoints being expressed—and heard! The second point is that in an area of uncertainty, especially where there is grave ignorance about the thresholds for irreversible change, it is necessary to set arbitrary standards and prudent to be conservative in the level at which they are pitched. With experience, these standards will inevitably be changed, but perhaps it will be better to move from a conservative, over-cautious posture to a more relaxed, more accurately researched standard.

The first and most obvious need is to establish on a world scale a proper system for monitoring the environment. As a result of the 1972 Stockholm Conference, the first tentative steps have been taken, but it would seem fair to remark that the resources currently and prospectively devoted to this enterprise are a minute fraction of those spent on observing and predicting the weather. Unless we establish a continuing Domesday survey, using the word as the Normans understood its meaning, we may end up as helpless spectators of our own day of Doom.

A closely related and urgent need is to establish much more precisely the nature of the economic and ecological trade-offs that are available. Because there are multiple criteria, it is not conceivable that a single "right" answer can be found. Since, in this sense, nobody can be "right", it would be folly if debate degenerated into a squabble, with everyone pointing out that everybody else is wrong. However, only if the available trade-offs are established can a proper discussion be held to decide which courses of action are considered more desirable (or less undesirable) than others. For example, those economists wedded to the notion that economic growth is a "good thing" might pause to ask themselves whether the time has not arrived when the greatest benefit to humanity might not arise from the maintenance and improvement of the world's environment. Galbraith (1958) wrote about private affluence amidst public squalor: perhaps his notion of public squalor ought to be broadened to include the whole ecosystem—of the world and not merely one nation. Thus, as the world's population grows and technology advances, perhaps an increasing share of real product must be devoted to the maintenance and improvement of the ecological "public goods". (Mishan, 1967; Brubacker, 1972.)

Finally, and closely related to the previous point, it is now abundantly clear that for certain environmental parameters it is essential that standards, preferably conservative and even stringent ones, must be laid down with a view to protecting the Earth's life systems. The United States has taken a firm line over the emission of exhaust fumes from motor vehicles. In Britain, we have cleaned up the atmosphere of most cities, have made considerable progress in cleaning our rivers and are about to embark on a programme that should eliminate the discharge of raw sewage into the estuaries and coastal waters. Earlier in the post-war period, international action was taken regarding the level of atmospheric strontium resulting from nuclear tests. It is quite conceivable that in a country where farming is as intensive as it is in Britain, standards will have to be set for the maximum rates of fertilizer application: excess nitrogen in rivers and lakes is associated with excess growth of aquatic vegetation leading to asphyxia for fishes; similarly, excess nitrogen in groundwater supplies has been linked with jaundice in new-born infants. The imposition of standards inevitably will arouse the opposition of groups adversely affected. The more powerful these groups are, the greater the need for a public (national and international) awareness of the issues involved.

You will have noted that I have concentrated on questions relating to pollution. The reason is that in my opinion it is in this area that the greatest hazards lie. However, it would be wrong to imply that there are no problems of significance relating to food supplies and the stock of non-renewable minerals. Just the reverse. My stand on these issues is essentially that the predictable operations of the market system to deal with long-term changes in the relative prices of resources, and of governments to ensure adequate supplies of food for their populations, will suffice. On the last point, it is becoming clear that the nations of the world must individually and collectively adopt population policies— something which it is only now becoming respectable to talk about as applying to Britain with as much force as nations comprising the Third World.

At the end of the day, I am cautiously optimistic, provided that the debate is a debate and not a slanging match. To borrow a phrase, if it is true that "protection of the environment is an economic problem for which economics has no ready answers" (Richardson, 1971), it is equally truly a problem for many other disciplines for which they also do not have ready answers. Thus, just as the Food and Agriculture Organization has played a leading role in monitoring the progress of agricultural production in the world, it is my hope that the United Nations, following the Stockholm Conference, will take a lead in compiling and publishing statistics on world resources of all kinds. Meantime, perhaps the Central Statistical Office in this country could complement the *Annual Abstract of Statistics* and *Social Trends* with a companion volume on *Resource Trends*, covering data on atmospheric, river and sea pollution, the consumption of minerals and production of waste materials that need to be dumped, etc. But the collection and publication of information is only a beginning. Much more important is an imaginative approach to the problems of international co-operation. For example, within Britain, we have a Redundancies Payment Fund to compensate workers whose jobs disappear through no fault of their own. Is there not a case for an analogous international fund, whereby nations that are especially affected adversely by limitations on the use of resources or the emission of pollutants could be compensated, at least for an interim period? An example of a situation which might be easier to resolve were such a fund to exist is provided by the dispute between Iceland on the one hand and Britain, Germany and other fishing nations, on the other. To protect the stock of fish against over-fishing, Iceland unilaterally extended her territorial seas to 50 miles from the mainland. It might have been easier to reach agreement on controlling the total catch and thereby avoiding the international imbroglio that developed in 1972, if those parties adversely affected could be compensated. Payments into the fund might be on either or both of two bases:

1. in proportion to total Gross National Product, weighted by income per person. The richer nations would pay proportionately more than the poorer;
2. a tax levied on the consumption of resources for which there is good reason to believe that supplies will not last for more than a few decades.

The justice might be rough-and-ready, the bureaucracy clumsy, but some kind of arrangement along these lines seems to be urgently needed. At the national level there are precedents to follow; Canada makes payments to salmon fishers for not engaging in their pursuit. So why not international action along the same lines?

References

Beckerman, W. (1972). Economists, scientists and environmental catastrophe. *Oxford Economic Papers, New Series*, **24**, 327–344.

Brubacker, S. (1972). *To Live on Earth: Man and his Environment in Perspective*. Baltimore: Johns Hopkins Press.

The Ecologist (1972). **2**, 1.

Galbraith, J. K. (1958). *The Affluent Society*. London: Hamish Hamilton.

Maddox, J. (1972). *The Doomsday Syndrome*. London: Macmillan.

Mishan, E. J. (1967). *The Costs of Economic Growth*. London: Staples Press.

Richardson, H. W. (1971). Economics and the environment. *Quart. Rev. Nat. Westminster Bank*, May, 43–52.

Royal Commission on Environmental Pollution (1972). *Third Report*. London: H.M.S.O., Cmnd. 5054.

Water Resources:
Future Prospects

BARRY RYDZ

Water Resources Board, Reading, England

The theme of this symposium is the comparison of population and resources; that is to say, how are we to stretch our resources to meet the needs of an expanding and constantly more demanding population?

Unfortunately I am not able to present a global perspective of world water needs and resources, which is something probably expected of me; I do not have the data of all the continents at my command nor do I think that anybody yet has a comprehensive grasp of all the relevant aspects of water balance. We are only beginning, in the more industrialized countries, to make meaningful assessments of the balance of demand and resources, which in many cases is not nearly as simple as might appear at first sight.

However, I hope that I shall be able to give a greater insight into the sort of problems that are involved and how they are being considered and I will illustrate my remarks mainly by reference to England and Wales simply because that is the area for which my Board has some responsibility and an area for which it is convenient to present figures.

I propose to discuss mainly the use of the fresh water that is left with us in the course of the natural water cycle. About one part in a thousand of the earth's hydrological cycle probably passes through England and Wales. On the other hand, we have at the present time rather more than 1 per cent of the world's population and we are likely to have nearly 1 per cent in the closing years of this century. In that simple sense it might be thought that the problems of water resource development are as taxing here as in most places. There is rather more to the story than that as will, I hope, become apparent. But for that reason the area of England and Wales is of some relevance for illustration.

Before discussing the usual methods of exploiting the water cycle I should like briefly to mention two subjects that are somewhat extraneous to the traditional approach. The first is the possibility of weather modification, which has had some attention in the United States. It is there estimated that about 10 per cent of the atmospheric water passing over the continent is actually precipitated and that something could well be done to get at the other 90 per cent. Experiments have been conducted over 20 or 25 years, and in some areas, particularly in the South-West, it has been found possible to increase the net precipitation by about 10 or 15 per cent. This may only involve the transfer of precipitation from one place to another, but that can be valuable in itself.

The second is the de-salting of sea water, about which we hear a great deal. Although there are many plants in service in various parts of the world their total output would probably only about equal the needs of London, so that this source is still very minor in the context of world requirements. Its costs are still very high and, compared with the costs of developing natural supplies in this country, rapidly disappearing in the wrong direction. Contrary to what many were expecting five or ten years ago, the cost gap has widened greatly in recent years.

This method of attempting to imitate the natural cycle with a do-it-yourself system is also a way of making unnecessary inroads into fuel reserves and into the assimilative capacity of the environment for waste heat and polluting residues. If we converted wholesale to baseload, single purpose distillation plant for water supply in this country, we should require quantities of energy of the same order as those that we are now using for electricity production. We should also require unsightly plants along much of our coastline. It is thus a step that we should contemplate very seriously before embarking upon it unnecessarily. It has often surprised me that people who consider themselves conservationists and who regard reservoirs as a serious environmental affliction sometimes press this alternative, which in all these important respects would be that much more costly.

The first thing to emphasize about water as a resource is that it is renewable; it has this much in common with some other resources which will be discussed today. However, there is one respect in which it is unique; it is not only renewable but for most of its uses it is re-usable, theoretically to an almost infinite extent. The things we do with water rarely affect it chemically, although minute amounts are used in water of crystallization, liquid products and so on. In this country, broadly speaking, we use it to carry heat, to carry waste and to carry raw materials and materials in process; having done this it can in the right circumstances nearly all be made available for another use.

There is an important exception, of course, which is not a chemical change but a change of state. Some of the water we use is sent back to the atmosphere, either by irrigation, as in many countries, or, as in this country, by evaporation for cooling purposes. I must emphasize the fundamental distinction in this respect when considering the adequacy of water resources between countries that have a substantial consumptive (invariably an irrigation) requirement, and countries such as this one, most of eastern North America and Western Europe, that do not. Their problems are fundamentally different not only in scale but in nature.

Roughly half of the precipitation we get in this country is transpired or evaporated naturally before the residue reaches rivers or underground rock formations. The proportion varies a great deal from place to place. In some other parts of the world much less than half, and in others very much more than half, disappears in this way. In the continental United States, for instance, about two-thirds vanishes before it can be used. Even in this country there are wide variations in this respect.

Figure 1 indicates the residual rainfall for England and Wales. The precipitation on England and Wales varies from over 3,000 mm in parts of the West to as little as 500 mm in the fens and around the Thames Estuary. Potential evaporation ranges from less than, say, 400 mm to more than 500 mm, with a gradient opposite to that of the rainfall variation. There are substantial areas in the West where on average about 2,000 mm of residual rainfall are available to feed our rivers whilst in the fens and most of Essex virtually nothing would be left if the potential evaporation were always realised. As actual summer evapotranspiration is nearly always less than potential in these drier areas, a few inches are left. There is thus a tremendously steep gradient in the graph of resources in those terms.

I should mention that the information on which the above figures and our resource calculations are based has almost all been obtained within the past century. If it should prove untypical or if there were to be even a slight shift in, say, the balance of winter and summer rainfall—in a word, if we were dealing with a non-stationary series of events—this might have very considerable effects on our resource potential and on such things as our storage requirements.

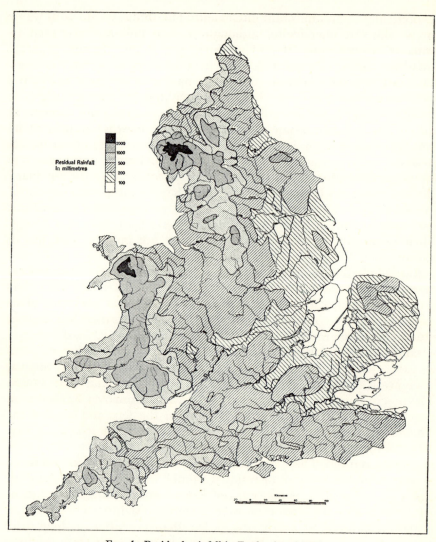

Fig. 1. Residual rainfall in England and Wales.

I have suggested that in industrial countries a great deal of water is re-used. This is a fundamental distinction which we must always have in mind when discussing the adequacy of resources. In England and Wales for instance, we have residual rainfall equivalent to about 200 million cubic metres a day. It varies greatly from time to time, but on average that is about the figure. "Use" may be defined in a great variety of ways and this is one of the problems in water resource assessment and development. But more than half of that amount is used in the sense that the total of water that passes through domestic taps and industrial processes and the condensers of power stations is probably well in excess of 100 million cubic metres a day. There is another definition of "use" and that is the amount that is withdrawn from rivers and aquifers. In this country that amounts to between 40 million and 50 million cubic metres a day, about a quarter of the total of residual rainfall. There are other convenient definitions but the ultimate definition of consumption, in the sense of water which is evaporated or incorporated in products, brings it down to less than a million cubic metres a day in this country, or $\frac{1}{2}$ per cent of our total resources. It is unlikely that even by the end of the century this will rise far beyond 1 per cent.

However, the estimates of total use and even of total withdrawal given above are many times greater than the combined natural dry-weather flows of our rivers. In some instances, successive abstractions from industrial rivers amount to between ten and twenty times their dry weather flow and are in effect maintained by multiple re-use of the natural flow plus the effluents contributed, via the sewage works, from storage-based public water supply systems.

Thus, in countries of this kind the water resource problem can only be understood in the dynamic sense of maintaining a balance between the various elements of water storage, use and re-use and effluent treatment. The measure of our resources, what they are worth, is inseparably bound up with consideration of the ways in which we are to use them, the locations of our factories, and the treatments we apply. Where irrigation is the dominant use, on the other hand, comparatively simple equations can sometimes be drawn up between resources and needs.

The residual rainfall over the 48 contiguous United States is probably about 4,500 million cubic metres a day. Like us, the Americans withdraw about one-quarter and by the end of the century will be withdrawing, and in that simple sense using, one-half to two-thirds of that amount. But an important difference is that, averaged over that vast area, between 5 and 10 per cent of the residual rainfall is now consumed and at the end of the century probably more than 10 per cent will be consumed.

An extreme case is to be found in the American South-West, in states such as California, for instance. Withdrawals are now probably two-thirds or three-quarters of the available natural input, but of this the greater part is applied to crops and evaporated. It is likely that by the end of the century rather more than half of the natural endowment of residual rainfall in California and all the neighbouring States will be evaporated in this way.

At this stage of the process we reach a plateau of development in areas of that kind, in that it is doubtful whether irrigation can be further extended except by radically more expensive measures. These have been given much attention. One hears of plans in North America to tap the resources of the Columbia River, of parts of Canada and of Alaska and to convey the water to California. Already there are developments in California which are conveying water for the better part of 1,000 miles, and the main canal carrying water southwards under the current State water project conveys an amount about equal to three-quarters of our abstractions from rivers in England and Wales for all purposes.

There are of course other areas, in Asia, Africa and Australia, where water storage, transfer and consumptive use are developed on a very large scale. Schemes have been mooted for diverting the northward flowing rivers of Siberia, and the Brahmaputra, to irrigate the heartlands of Asia. These are proposals for which the technical resources could, I believe, eventually be found if it became a question of survival. They would be immensely expensive expedients. Nevertheless, it may be surmised that there will be a more pressing need for them than for some of the projects which now swallow up our resources, and one day they may have to be tackled.

Before we tackle them, however, attention must surely be given to the relative economics of producing more food in areas that require a great deal of irrigation and of producing greater amounts in those areas that are naturally well watered. In the United States, for instance, food production is made possible in parts of Arizona at a very high irrigation cost, whilst it is limited in other areas more favoured by nature. Because there are not only economic but serious political obstacles to moving water across continents, questions like these are likely to demand answers before some of these plans come to fruition. But undoubtedly great freshwater resources remain to be tapped, even without bringing into the argument the modification of the weather cycle, the large-scale production of fresh water from the sea and the use of polar ice, all of which almost certainly have some potential. In Alaska, for instance, there are freshwater resources equal to about a half of those in the 48 contiguous United States, and, in the Amazon basin, quantities much larger still.

I now turn to the very different needs of countries such as Britain, the countries of Western Europe and the eastern States and provinces of North America. In doing this we are exchanging the vast storage and transfer projects which have fascinated many water engineers and statesmen since the dawn of history, and in the story of which the rise and fall of some ancient civilizations can be traced, for the less exciting but more subtle and demanding study of the interaction of water quantity and water quality problems in the humid industrialized areas. However, I should first like to refer to three basic ingredients of water resource development.

The first is storage to carry water over from periods of plenty to periods of shortage. The storage reservoirs provided in this country usually hold enough water to be drawn upon, without complete refilling, through either a single dry summer or through two successive dry summers and the intervening winter, and they are refilled during the next winter. No substantial river basin is equipped with artificial storage representing more than about thirty days' mean river flow and the average for England and Wales is eight or nine days. In other countries, particularly in the more arid areas, much more extensive balancing storage has been provided. An extreme example is to be found on the Colorado River which is now provided with reservoir storage equivalent to between two and three years' flow and in theory capable of balancing the vagaries of river flow over decades. Indeed, in this case the point has been reached at which any supplement to dry weather flow resulting from greater storage would be outweighed by increased evaporation from the surface of the storage.

The total artificial storage in England and Wales—equivalent to about eight to nine days of mean residual rainfall over the whole country —will probably have to be doubled by the end of the century if we are to make ends meet. By contrast, the 48 United States already have storage equivalent to about 100 days' mean run off for their combined area (in volume, nearly three hundred times as much as we have) and during this century will require roughly to double that. This partly reflects the greater availability of storage areas in the U.S., for instance for flood control; but in the main it is an indication of two things—the comparatively equable nature of the British climate and, largely as a result of that, the much less demanding, non-consumptive nature of our water needs as compared with several areas of the U.S. and, indeed, much of the rest of the world.

The second main ingredient of water resource development is the means for conveying water from one place to another; pipelines, tunnels, regulated rivers and so on. Storage is a means of distribution in time; conveyance is a means of distribution in space, and one for which our geography and our density of development create special opportunities in England and Wales.

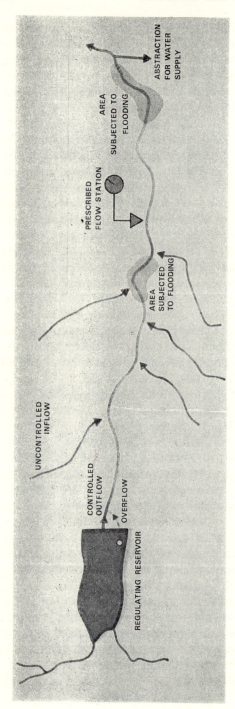

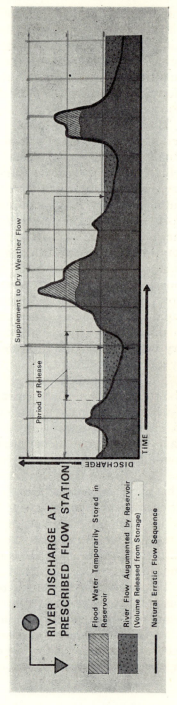

Fig. 2. River regulation.

The third major ingredient is treatment. This includes treatment of clean water for drinking purposes, but more relevant in this respect is the treatment of effluents. In countries such as ours, there is in principle some choice between increasing the amount of storage and increasing the scope of treatment. In the Thames basin abstractions for water supply in the lower reaches already depend on the support of effluents produced higher up and this will be increasingly true in future. This depends on careful quality control. In other areas, for instance the Trent, we are considering whether the substantial input of effluent in the upper reaches can be reclaimed for public supply lower down by suitable patterns of effluent and water treatment and of general river management; already extensively re-used by industry. But in many areas the provision of more storage is the only safe and practical answer at this time.

Figure 2 indicates the system of river regulation. Storage is now being contemplated mainly for river regulation purposes; water released from storage near the head waters of rivers may be used to augment flow in dry periods, a proportion being abstracted just above the tidal reaches. This contrasts with the practice which became traditional in this country in the nineteenth century, when water trapped in upland reservoirs was conveyed to towns in pipes and only rejoined the river system from sewage outfalls, often in the lower reaches of another river. For obvious reasons, river regulation has environmental advantages as well as giving a greatly increased yield from a given volume of storage and providing some opportunities to mitigate flooding. In view of the improved ability to treat polluted water we are turning more and more to this approach.

The lower diagram on Fig. 2, in which river flow is plotted against time, shows what has to be done by storage. The periods of deficiency are the low parts of the curve which represents dry summers. These can be made up to a higher level by detaining some of the surplus winter flows in storage.

It is clear from the diagram that one gets diminishing returns from successive increments of storage, since in order to add a given supplement to dry weather flows—represented by a given vertical interval on the diagram—one has to supplement the flow, from storage, during increasingly long periods. Eventually the storage has to be used to supplement flows over a dry winter, as well as during the adjacent summers, and subsequently over several winters. This eventually sets an economic limit to the provision of storage.

By plotting the minimum accumulated natural inflow which can be relied upon during periods of varying duration we can determine what supplement from storage is needed over a period to maintain any required level of output (Fig. 3). But strictly speaking this minimum natural flow is indeterminate; we may provide enough storage to meet the worst situation on record, although more usually we try to provide enough to reduce the risk of failure to some theoretically predetermined value (say, 1 per cent or 2 per cent probability). It is important to realize that all designs to balance the irregularities of natural rainfall merely purport to reduce to some supposedly acceptable level the risk that supplies will fall below our needs in a very dry year; a run of many

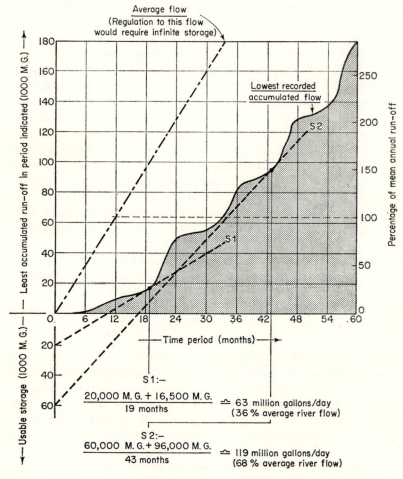

Fig. 3. Lowest accumulated flow diagram: storage needed for balancing.

wet or near average years, as recently experienced in this country, may do nothing to prove the adequacy or otherwise of our provision.

One may plot such curves of minimum reliable flow in dimensionless terms, as percentages of average flow. A family of such curves, for areas of different rainfall, shows that, broadly speaking, those catchments which are least well supplied with rainfall also have the most variable rainfall and flow characteristics. The problems of dry areas are therefore compounded by the relative unreliability of rainfall, and even more of flow, in these areas. In the dry South-West of the United States the annual flow which can be relied on in 19 years out of 20 is as low as 25 per cent of the long average whereas in the North-East it is nearly 70 per cent. This helps to explain the enormous disparity between storage needs in well watered and in drier areas.

Figure 4 shows the 29 river authority areas in England and Wales. It indicates the amounts distributed through public water supply systems as fractions of the residual rainfall in each of the areas, that is to say, of the natural endowment of each area. The diagram shows that this form of use represents only a tiny fraction of the natural resource in western areas, but increases in relative size in the drier and more populous areas until, in the case of the Lee Conservancy, one of our smallest river authorities, the situation is reversed, and the amount distributed in that area, simply through the public supply, already exceeds the whole of the amount with which nature has endowed it, and the area can survive only by import. The amalgamation of these areas into larger units would of course somewhat even out these discrepancies. But even for the ten large regional water authority areas now proposed the ratio of current public water supply within the area to average residual rainfall will vary from about 35 per cent (Regional Water Authority No. 6) to 2 per cent (Wales: Regional Water Authority No. 10), rising by the end of this century to 55 per cent and 4 per cent, respectively. For England and Wales as a whole the total supplied through public mains now represents about 7 per cent of average residual rainfall and by the end of the century this will probably reach between 13 per cent and 15 per cent. This gives a rough picture of how we stand in comparing ultimate resources with that very important form of use in this country. How far we can approach the ultimate in terms of developed use depends, of course, on availability of storage.

The public supplies now available are mainly drawn from storage reservoirs or from underground sources which, by lowering the water table during prolonged dry periods, effectively make use of storage underground; after use they give rise to sewage effluents which

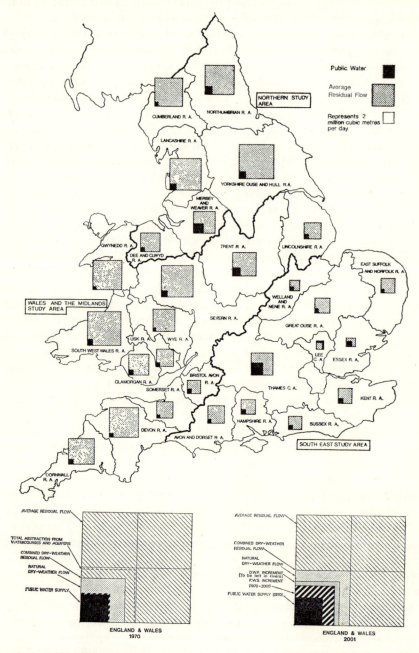

Fig. 4. Natural water resources and public supplies in England and Wales, 1970.

supplement the natural flows of rivers. These natural flows also derive, after a long period of dry weather, from storage in soils and rocks. The greater irregularity of rainfall in the drier areas, and hence of accumulated flows over long dry spells, further accentuates the problems of our eastern river basins (such as the proposed RWA No. 6) as compared with areas in the west. But this handicap is partially offset, especially over short rainless periods, by the fortunate circumstance which has placed most of our water-bearing rock formations in these drier areas.

The lower diagram in Fig. 4 shows (to the same scale as the river authority symbols) the total natural dry weather flow of English and Welsh rivers and the supplement to it from storage in reservoirs etc. in relation to total average flow or residual rainfall. Together they amount to perhaps one-sixth of this average. The projection to the year 2000 shows a combination of storage effects, natural and man-made, which will build up dry weather flows to about one-quarter of this average, including (if this should prove necessary) a direct supplement from new reservoir storage to the residual dry weather flow in the lower courses of rivers and into estuaries.

In recent studies the Water Resources Board have sought to identify reservoir and estuary storage sites and areas in which storage in underground rocks can be exploited by intermittent pumping techniques so as to regulate rivers. The storage thus identified amounts to about four times that likely to be required by about the end of this century. If these developments prove broadly acceptable, this country can balance its needs probably until well into the next century by means of this kind. Of course, in this crowded island it is likely that every one of these sites will involve some degree of social conflict, and one cannot predict what the priorities of future generations will be. But it is fair to say that the sites I have referred to would not involve problems any more severe than those involved in the reservoir promotions of recent decades, and the area of land involved would be a minute fraction of that likely to be needed for other development purposes.

The Water Resources Board are now preparing a report in which they will recommend suitable patterns of water resource development in England and Wales for the next generation. They may well select a comparatively small number of sites for large reservoirs combined, possibly, with some of the developments in estuaries which have been studied for this purpose (Morecambe Bay, the Dee and the Wash) in order to meet needs for the next 30 years. I think that about 2,000 million cubic metres of new storage will be needed in reservoirs and estuaries during that time, occupying up to 35,000 acres in all. Much of this, probably the greater part, can be in the inter-tidal areas of estuaries or on sites already partly occupied by storage reservoirs. Among other things the new water space will help to meet recreational needs which in the view of some forecasters threaten to be insatiable. But first the maximum use is likely to be made of water in underground storage and in due course it may prove possible to add to this by re-charging surface water into aquifers; for instance, into the depleted aquifer of the London Basin.

In assessing the extent of developments in public water supply which are likely to be necessary during the remainder of this century we have relied on estimates of population and extrapolation of historical records of *per capita* use, or in certain cases, extrapolation of the recorded amounts of water supplied to the home and to industry from public water systems. It is thought likely, for instance, that the present per capita daily use of some 290 litres from the public supply, of which some two thirds is domestic use, will grow to between 450 and 500 litres by the turn of the century. All the ingredients of such forecasts are liable to errors either way and, as we all know, estimates of future population in this country have been rather sharply revised during the past few years. But our planning horizon of 2001 is an arbitrary one and the uncertainty in demand projection is most conveniently regar-ded as uncertainty about the date at which growing demands are likely to pass through the forecast level. Since the main purpose of our forward estimating is to test alternative patterns of development rather than to predict future demand levels for their own sake an error of ± 5 years in the date of the so-called "2001" demand is not of great significance, provided that the sensitivity of choices of strategy to variations in the growth of demand and, indeed, in other uncertain factors is tested in appropriate ways.

In any case uncertainties about future industrial technology and plant location, with their implications for direct river water use by riparian industries, may prove to be of much greater consequence. It is in this field that assessment of the future quantitative balance is most open to challenge and, indeed, merges with the problems of quality maintenance and of the disposal of waterborne wastes. Our projections for England and Wales have assumed a very considerable extension of re-use of river water for industrial purposes and of internal recycling, especially for cooling. Very little storage development has been allowed for over and above that required for the expansion of public water supply.

Compared with most other populous countries, such as our European neighbours, we have a rather low residual rainfall per head of the population, equivalent to about 4,000 litres per head of the population per day. On the other hand, our unusually equable rainfall means that a little storage goes a long way, and we are in a good position to network water about the country in rivers and aqueducts provided that we can take advantage of our short internal lines of communication. So much for the quantitative balance; what is now becoming more important is the qualitative balance—the means we use to maintain and restore water quality throughout the river system, not simply in order to extend our resources by re-use, but in order to help bring the environments of our industrial areas up to the standards we should now be willing to afford. For this there will have to be a great expansion in the third ingredient of water resource management I mentioned; effluent treatment. We have in this country fairly small rivers with very limited assimilative capacity for effluents, but, on the other hand, comparatively ready access to the sea.

In these respects each of the industrialized countries has its special problems. In some of them the problems of water pollution are entering an acute phase, whereas there is reason to hope that our worst problems in this field lie behind us. But as a broad generalization, taking quantity and quality together, it would be reasonable to suppose that the prospects of our European neighbours and of other similar countries are no more forbidding, and in many cases rather easier, than our own.

Professor Chisholm has mentioned in his introductory chapter the publication of information and the interchange of ideas. This is most important. The Water Resources Board has made it a plank of its policy in the past seven or eight years to broadcast as wide an array of water resource alternatives as possible, to explain their merits and difficulties and to bring a wide circle of interests into their discussion. It is important that that should continue. We are entering a new phase of water reorganization in which the present Board is coming to an end and it is not yet clear how this open approach will be maintained. I hope that it will be, because to retreat from it would be a retrograde step.

It is also important to improve the procedures for interdisciplinary liaison in the selection, design and management of water projects. Water engineers and, one hopes, others whose work brings about major changes in the environment are increasingly aware of the need for this. I was in Paris recently for a study group, initiated by water management people under the auspices of the Organization for Economic Co-operation and Development (OECD), to appraise their own efforts in this direction and to generate ideas for more effective co-operation with ecologists and others who see the environmental

B

impact of proposals in a different light. Experience (for instance, in the studies of estuary storage in this country) has shown that there is room for fruitful co-operation and adjustment of plans over a wide field, even though some ultimate priorities remain for resolution at the political level. But efforts must be made from all sides to bridge the gaps, and this means willingness to engage in a constructive dialogue. The starting point for this must be mutual trust in our sense of responsibility to the public we serve. I should be glad to hear of any suggestions for improving mutual confidence and co-operation in these fields.

I hope my paper will help to bring into focus the extent and nature of water resource problems for the next few generations. It is not for me to say how they compare in urgency with other resource problems, but I fancy that for this country and perhaps for most others a close approach to resource limits, with the consequent agonising reappraisals, will come earlier in some other fields. We can force the pace of adjustment in water use, as in any other field of development and in the consumption of almost any other commodity, by imposing controls: water rationing or taxation. Without going this far we can perhaps try to reflect in the supply price of water a "social cost" element; but again this is true of many other commodities and services, including some which are sold wholly by measure and others which, like water, are not. It would be odd if water were singled out for this treatment simply because so much challenging thinking about resource economics has recently found expression in the water field.

Human Calorie and Protein Needs and How Far They are Satisfied Today

P. V. SUKHATME

Gokhale Institute of Politics and Economics, Poona, India

Introduction

Part of the population in the developing countries admittedly does not get enough to eat to meet the energy needs for a healthy active life, and an even larger part does not get food of the right quality. Estimates of the malnourished have varied widely in the past, from two-thirds to a negligible proportion. In a paper which the author presented to the Royal Statistical Society (1961), and in a survey based on the results thereof, it was estimated that some 10 to 15 per cent of the people in the world, or roughly 20 per cent of the people in the developing countries, did not meet their energy needs during the decade 1950–1960, (they were undernourished). The study was extended to estimate the incidence of protein deficiency as data became available; this estimate was placed at between 25 and 33 per cent (Sukhatme, 1966).

What has since become clear is that protein deficiency is for the most part the indirect result of inadequate energy intake. In other words, what diets lack is energy foods to avoid the body katabolizing the protein people do eat (Gopalan, 1968). This finding is the opposite of what has been reported in various studies of the subject, notably the study on protein gap by the U.N. Committee on Application of Science and Technology to Development (U.N. 1968), which has formed the basis for international action. So serious is the shortfall in protein, according to the U.N. Report, and so adverse are the effects of protein malnutrition, that it gave a warning that the physical and mental development of future generations could become completely arrested unless prompt action was taken to help countries raise protein levels in the diets of children. Countries were accordingly urged to set up machinery, at the highest level, to promote and produce protein food using modern technology to avoid the impending crisis (U.N. Resolution 2319).

The finding that protein deficiency is indirectly caused by low calorie intake is gradually being confirmed by a number of workers and is also reflected in the recent writings of FAO (1971). Yet by and large it continues to be ignored in international and national action. It would appear, to quote Hegsted:

> that entrepreneurs and enterprisers have combined together to transfer protein technology to developing countries even before people have time to appraise the facts.

Perhaps the finding is too revolutionary to be believed. Be that as it may, it is clearly important and opportune that once again we should make an objective appraisal of the extent of hunger and malnutrition in the world. I shall briefly review what are man's needs for calories and protein before proceeding with the evaluation of the data to ascertain how far human needs are satisfied today.

Calorie and Protein Needs

Assessing human needs for calories and protein has been the subject of continuous investigation both at international and national levels. The task has proved difficult not only because of the inherent difficulties in defining requirements for health but also because of lack of adequate data on human subjects. Nevertheless, thanks to the lead by FAO and WHO, requirements already developed (FAO, 1957a; FAO/WHO, 1965) have received approval wide enough to warrant their use for evaluating the adequacy of food supply and its distribution in the population.

For calories, the requirements are defined as average *per caput* needs of a specified age-sex group. It is recognized that individuals within a group may need calories which may be below or above the suggested average but the principal concern is with establishing averages and not with variation within groups. All that is stated about variation is that most adult men would appear to have a daily expenditure requiring between 2400–4000 calories, implying a standard deviation of approximately 400 calories. It is emphasized that the averages are intended for application to large groups and are not intended for the individual, presumably because little is known about the form of distribution of requirements.

For protein, the requirements are based on consideration of the individual as well as of the group and are defined at three levels, namely, average, average $+20$ per cent and average -20 per cent. The upper level, which is placed at a distance of twice the standard deviation above the average protein needs, is expected to cover the requirements of all but a very small proportion of the population. In other words, the probability that a healthy individual will have a requirement exceeding the upper level will be very small. The lower level is placed at twice the standard deviation below the average and represents the level, in all but a few individuals, below which protein deficiency may be expected to occur. In other words, the probability that a healthy individual will have a protein need below the lower level will be very small. The magnitude of individual variability is estimated at 10 per cent.

An example is given in Table I which shows the recommended requirements for a pre-school child and adult living in India, based on FAO and WHO studies (1957b, 1965) and the recommendation of the Indian Council of Medical Research (1968).

TABLE I

Recommended levels of nutrient intake for the pre-school child and adult in India (approximations only)

Age	Cal.	Protein as egg in g*	%Prot./Cal. concentration	% Prot./Cal. concentration when N.P.U. relative to egg is 67
1—3 years	1,000	12·0	4·8	7·2
Adult male	2,700	33·0	4·8	7·2

* Defined as average$+20\%$.

These recommendations for calories and protein have been recently reviewed (FAO/WHO, 1971). They are still in press but are already being applied by FAO in its work (*vide* FAO, 1971). A brief account of these recommendations is also given in the FAO report on commodity projections. The new recommendations are naturally a little different from those formulated earlier, based as they are on the best knowledge at present available. Briefly, compared with the previous data, the energy requirements have been slightly increased for children up to 10 years of age, but reduced markedly for adolescent boys and girls. Further, according to current observations for a moderately active "reference" male adult weighing 65 kg the require-metns are reduced from 3,200 to 3,000 calories, and for an adult female from 2,300 to 2,200 calories. The general effect of these revisions on average *per caput* calorie requirement for the population is small.

For protein, recommendations for pre-school children have been increased but those for adults cut down. On the other hand, the practice of defining requirements at three levels has been given up. The current practice is to define the requirements at the upper level of the range of requirements. It is called the recommended intake or allowance. The meaning remains the same; namely, that the requirements of most healthy individuals will be met by less than the recommended intake. The magnitude of individual variability has been revised upwards from 10 to 15 per cent. The effect of these revisions generally is small.

Protein-requirement estimates have not received the same degree of acceptance as calorie requirements. The principal reservation against them is that they are too low compared with what people eat in the rich countries. However, the recent review should help to dispel this reservation, because the requirements have been corrected for bias and brought into line with the results based on the consumption of actual protein. This improves their acceptability. At the same time, the results of feeding experiments with the actual protein show that the protein quality of diet relative to eggs is higher than was previously assumed. The net effect of the 1971 revision is thus to make the require-ments per person per day even lower than the previous estimates made by FAO. The explanation of the large gap between intake and require-ments in the rich countries appears to be that people with high and rising incomes must find it difficult not to eat more, especially tasty animal foods, when they can afford to do so.

There is one further point about requirements. There is a general belief that a child needs much more protein in relation to his energy needs than does an adult. This is, however, not borne out on current evidence which shows that if a diet has 5 per cent of its calories from good quality protein, such as in egg or milk, the individual's needs for protein will be met regardless of whether he is a pre-school child or an adult man, provided he eats enough to meet his energy needs. Since most diets are known to have more than the equivalent of 5 per cent good quality protein, we may expect a child's needs usually to be met. Where, however, a diet consists predominantly of starchy roots like cassava or tapioca, it is possible that the concentration and quality of protein in the diet may turn out to be inadequate. Such cases will in general be too few to be ascribed to the shortfall in protein supply. Such diets are, however, sometimes given to a pre-school child during transition from weaning to solid diet and especially when he is unwell, and this is precisely the time when he requires a supplement of good quality protein. Even cereal-based diets with small supplements of legumes may turn out to be inadequate when a child is unwell, such as after an attack of diarrhoea, because he may not eat enough to meet his energy needs. This need not, however, be interpreted to mean that a child's needs for protein should be met from protein-rich foods to prevent protein malnutrition; even breast milk contains only 5 or 6 per cent of calories from protein, and it is an ideal infant food. So children are more demanding than adults in their requirements, and it is easier to meet these requirements with good foods like eggs and milk if one can afford them. These are good not only because they contain good quality protein, but also because they are concentrated sources of energy, vitamins, and minerals. These are however, largely questions of nutrition education, and are outside the scope of this paper.

How Far are the Needs Satisfied Today ?

Macro-analysis

Table II shows the current levels of energy and protein supply *per caput* compared with respective requirements region by region. In view of the emphasis on the word "today" in the title, the estimates for 1962 and 1965 have been also included in the Table. The estimates are based on the food balance sheets for the countries prepared by FAO WHO (1970). As is well known they are subject to various sources of error but space does not permit their discussion beyond stating that a great deal of effort has gone into improving them in recent years. In particular, concepts and definitions have been standardized and accurate methods of estimating production, particularly of foodgrain crops, which contribute by far the major share to available calorie and protein supply, have been introduced in many of the developing countries. Extensive field checks carried out in a few countries show that while such estimates cannot by any means be claimed to be unbiased they would nevertheless appear to be accurate enough to indicate differences in time of the order of 5 per cent.

It will be seen that energy supplies for all the less developed regions except one fall short of the respective requirements by 5 to 10 per cent. For Latin America, they exceed average needs by about 5 per cent. For the less developed countries as a whole the supplies are short of needs by about 5 per cent. The table also shows that in all regions over the last decade there is a distinct though modest improvement in calorie level in relation to requirement. Clearly, the current programmes for

TABLE II

Food supplies: calories and proteins per caput compared with respective requirements

Regions	Calories				Proteins				Animal Proteins		
	Supplies			Require-ments	Supplies			Require-ments	Supplies		
	1962	1965	1970		1962	1965	1970		1962	1965	1970
Less Developed Regions	2,080	2,120	2,190	2,280	55·2	54·7	56·4	29·0	10·4	11·0	11·4
Asia and Far East (excluding China)	1,990	1,980	2,080	2,220	51·2	49·4	51·7	28·0	6·9	7·6	7·9
Near East	2,160	2,310	2,380	2,460	65·4	65·9	66·8	35·0	14·3	13·1	13·4
Africa	2,120	2,150	2,180	2,340	58·0	58·2	58·6	32·0	9·2	9·3	9·5
Latin America	2,350	2,470	2,520	2,380	61·4	63·7	64·9	29·0	22·4	23·7	24·7
Developed Regions*	3,010	3,090	3,150	2,560	86·4	90·7	92·2	30·0	43·1	46·9	50·9

* Including U.S.S.R. and Eastern Europe and excluding other Developed Countries.

TABLE III

Daily per caput calories and protein supply by expenditure level,
Maharashtra State, India, 1958

Expenditure in Rs./month	0—8	8—11	11—13	13—18	18—24	24—34	34—	Average
Total calories	1,120	1,560	1,850	2,190	2,440	2,530	3,340*	2,100
Total proteins(g)	30·7	45·0	52·8	60·4	66·3	71·7	85·7	59·7
Animal proteins (g)	1·0	1·8	2·3	2·9	6·1	7·1	11·9	4·5
Number of households	76	114	87	82	102	83	349	893

*This value appears unduly high. It is stated that this is partly due to the exclusion from the household size of guests and labourers taking meals.

TABLE IIIa

Daily per caput calories and protein supply by expenditure level,
Indonesia (Djawa–Madura), 1963–64

Expenditure in Rs./month	Less than 6,000	6,001– 10,000	10,001– 16,000	16,001– 30,000	30,001 and over	Average
Total calories	1,100	1,350	1,600	1,900	1,800	1,600
Total proteins (g)	18	23	29	36	37	29
Animal proteins (g)	3	4	7	9	14	7
Number of households	3,105	3,981	3,886	2,787	911	14,670

raising the high-yielding varieties of cereals, particularly wheat and rice, have made a distinct impact on the availability of food. If this trend continues, it may be expected that the calorie supply *per caput* should be about equal to the average needs in the course of the next 7 to 8 years.

Although the overall deficit is small, it needs to be interpreted with care, since within regions both calorie intake and the requirement vary considerably. The near self-sufficiency which the table shows is more apparent than real. Rich and privileged people everywhere eat all they need and more, but the poor only what they can afford—which may not always meet their needs. This is well brought out in Table III relating to India and Indonesia. While there is little doubt that consumption in Indonesia has been underestimated, with rising income the trend in the calorie consumption is unmistakably upwards. Clearly, an appreciable part of the population in the less developed countries must be undernourished.

For protein, far from a deficiency in the supply, there is a large excess. As Table II shows, the supply of protein *per caput* is nearly twice as large as the average requirement. Yet clinical surveys show that protein deficiency exists and is widespread: an appreciable part of the population is not getting adequate protein from the diet (Table III). However, a majority of these people also do not usually get adequate calories from the diet. As we shall see later, the protein deficiency which is reported from field surveys is evidently, for the most part, the indirect result of the inadequate energy intake.

TABLE IV

Per caput calorie and protein supplies by level of disposable income, U.S.A., 1965

Income $/year	Less than $3,000	$3,000–$4,999	$5,000–$6,999	$7,000–$9,999	$10,000 and over	All households
Calories	3,110	3,180	3,210	3,280	3,300	3,210
Proteins	98·1	102·4	106·7	109·5	112·9	105·8

By contrast, in developed countries there is no insufficiency of food, even in the poorest classes. Thus, Table IV shows that the calorie supply in the U.S.A., while increasing with income, is not appreciably influenced by rising income on anything like the scale noticed in poor countries like India or Indonesia. Further, for even the lowest income groups in the U.S.A., the level both of calorie and protein supply is seen to be higher than the respective average requirements.

Micro-analysis

Undernutrition

How far do the individual diets conform to the requirements for health and what in particular is the proportion of diets which can be considered as not satisfying calorie needs? In other words, what is the incidence of undernutrition in the population?

Ordinarily, in a healthy active population with each person meeting his exact requirements and assuming normal distribution, no more than 0·5 per cent of the individuals will have a calorie intake, on nutrition unit* basis, below the lower critical limit given by the average requirement of the "reference" man minus three times the standard deviation of an individual requirement. The average requirement of an adult male of "reference" type for a developing country such as India, is approximately 2,700 calories at the physiological level. The standard deviation is not known. However, if we assume that the requirement, is normally distributed, we can place it at 400 calories, as we did in our earlier studies based on the information that most people have energy expenditure in the range 2,400—4,000 calories. Consequently, in any observed distribution of intake, the proportion of individuals with calorie intake per nutrition unit falling below 1,500 (i.e. $2,700 - 3 \times 400$) may be considered to provide an estimate of the incidence of undernutrition in the population.

This was the method used in the previous studies of the incidence of hunger. But it was also observed that in actual fact the incidence may be larger since (a) one would expect *a priori* a positive correlation between intake and requirement, and (b) the form of distribution of requirement may not be normal. Available evidence indicates that the correlation between intake and requirement is small, even when the period of observation is as much as a week or longer (Edholm *et al.*, 1955, 1970). However, deviation from normality is likely to be large in view of the truncation that seems to exist at the lower end of the distribution. One method of allowing for it, due to Harries *et al.* (1961) is to adopt a realistic cut-off point such as at a distance of twice rather than thrice the standard deviation from the average requirement and using for standard deviation a value of 500 calories based on energy expenditure. In other words, the cut-off point will be 1,700 instead of 1,500. No refinement of this nature can be entirely satisfying but there can be no denying that it constitutes a great improvement over the earlier method. On the other hand available evidence indicates that when, as

* A nutrition unit for calories has the same requirements as those of the "reference" man.

in the developing countries, the intake is low the standard deviation is also lower, it would appear advisable to use for the standard deviation of requirement an estimate of 400 rather than 500 based on intake data for U.K. In other words the cut-off point might be placed at $2,700 - 2 \times 400$, i.e. 1,900.

There are good experimental grounds for supposing why, in fact, an intake of the order of 1,900 calories should constitute a minimum physiological limit for classification of a man as undernourished. It is well known that the metabolizable energy needed by man to maintain body content of heat is higher than the basal metabolizable rate (BMR). The latter represents the energy needed under resting and fasting conditions. Over and above it, a man will need to provide energy cost of specific dynamic action, of voluntary muscular activity for maintaining personal hygiene and of resynthesising tissue components which under fasting conditions will ordinarily be oxidized and lost to the body. The sum total of energy costs needed to maintain body content of heat is called energy for maintenance (C_m) and is experimentally found to be about one and a half times the energy needed for basal metabolism, i.e. $1.5 \times$ BMR. As an adult male of the "reference" type weighing 55 kg can be assumed to have BMR of approximately 1,300 calories, it follows that C_m can be placed at 1,900—2,000 calories. If a person is forced to adapt himself to an intake below this level he will be doing so either by reducing physical activity as far as possible, as children do, or by impairing functional capacity to absorb food and utilize dietary protein and reducing body weight in the process, or by reducing both the level of physical activity as well as body weight. In other words, a person with an intake below 1,900 to 2,000 per nutrition unit, besides being undernourished, will be susceptible to a state of protein malnutrition.

That this is the case is brought out admirably by data, shown in Table V, based on extensive series of short-term experiments on nitrogeneous balance in adults. It will be seen that when total calorie intake is limited but protein is not, there is a loss of body protein. As the calorie intake is increased the loss becomes progressively smaller. It is only when the calorie intake is adequate and above 1.5 times BMR that a man is found to utilize the protein fully in amounts needed to meet his body needs. Clearly, protein in the diet is partially diverted to meeting the calorie needs when the latter are not satisfied, thus exposing the person to the hazard of protein malnutrition. Incidentally, it is interesting to observe that protein in excess of body needs does not benefit the protein balance.

We are now in a position to examine intake distribution with a view to estimating the incidence of undernutrition in the developing countries. Available data are very meagre. This is understandable since food consumption surveys are a difficult and expensive undertaking. If the method of collection is simple, such as a one-time interview, one usually gets a good response, but it is hard to vouchsafe for the

TABLE V
Estimated protein loss (g/day) by an adult taking a diet restricted in protein or calories, or both

Protein	Calories per day				
(g/day)	900	1,600	2,200	2,800	3,200
0	45	42	40	40	40
20	30	23	21	20	20
40	30	12	—0	0	0
60	30	12	—0	0	+0

Source: based on Calloway and Spector (1954). *Am. J. clin. Nut.* **2.**

accuracy of the information; this can be improved by frequent visits and the use of objective methods but it is not easy to get households to cooperate and the method is too expensive. For these reasons, surveys to determine food intake are usually conducted in limited areas and cover the poorer sections of the population. Such data provide a valuable

TABLE VI
Distribution of households surveyed in India (Maharashtra State) 1958 by calorie supplies per day per reference man

Calories	%Frequency
Up to 1,300	6·8
1,300–1,700	9·7
1,700–2,100	14·7
2,100–2,500	16·3
2,500–2,900	16·6
2,900–3,300	12·9
3,300–3,700	9·0
3,700–4,100	5·5
4,100–4,500	3·5
4,500 and over	5·0
	100·0

source of information for analysing the causes of variation in intake, especially when they are combined within clinical and other investigations, but they cannot go so far as to provide an adequate basis for generalizing the extent of undernutrition in the world. Of necessity, therefore, we must restrict ourselves to illustrating the method on available data in the first instance.

Table VI gives one such illustrative distribution for the State of Maharashtra (India). The data were collected by interview, over a period of one month, in the course of the 14th round of the National Sample Survey of India, and they relate to a representative sample of 862 households. The survey gave an overall consumption estimated at 2,900 calories per nutrition unit at the retail level and a standard deviation of 1,100 calories.

Two features of the distribution shown in Table VI require attention. First, the distribution relates to households and not to individuals, and secondly it states calorie consumption at the retail and not at the physiological level. Clearly, we cannot apply the limit of 1,900 calories to calculate the proportion of undernourished. For households of 4 nutrition units on an average, the standard deviation of requirement per nutrition unit can be placed at approximately 200 calories. The corresponding cut-off point is therefore 2,700—2 × 200, i.e. 2,300 calories.

As for the difference between the retail and the physiological levels the general practice is to adopt a uniform allowance estimated at 5—7 per cent for the developing countries. However, for low intakes with which we are primarily concerned here the allowance will be much smaller and for all practical purposes can be assumed to be negligible. We may therefore not be far wrong in taking 2,300 calories as the cut-off point for calculating the incidence of undernutrition in Maharashtra. Accordingly reading from Table VI we see that 32 per cent of the households had a calorie intake below this value.

In all likelihood, the true incidence will be smaller than this value. First, the body weight of the "reference" man has been placed at 55 kg. This is rather high; available evidence points to a figure of 52 kg as a more realistic weight for Maharashtra giving, for cut-off point, a value of 2,200 instead of 2,300 calories and an incidence of 29 per cent. Secondly, unlike requirements which are measured by methods more directly physiological, calorie intake is measured using food composition tables and not laboratory analysis. Evidence available shows that when calorie intake is determined by chemical analysis the variation is lowered. To this we should add that the difference between the retail and the physiological levels will increase as the intake increases. It is therefore possible that at least a part of the difference between standard deviations of intake and requirement, estimated at 1,100 and 200 calories respectively for the data under examination, is apparent rather than real. Clearly this will result in overestimating the incidence of undernutrition though it is difficult to say by how much. All in all, considering the uncertainties of data, not only of requirements but of intake as well and the differences in the methods of measuring the two, it is impossible to find the dividing line with greater exactitude. We may conclude that between a quarter to a third of the households in Maharashtra were undernourished during 1958.

In earlier papers by FAO, data have been presented on the distribution of households by calorie intake per nutrition unit for a number of countries in Asia and the incidence of undernutrition in the population has been calculated following the method illustrated above for Maharashtra. They show that almost everywhere the overall calorie gap is small, but it is shared by a large proportion of the people, often as many as 50 per cent. There is, however, little point in presenting these data here as in most of the countries they covered only selected sections of the population, and there is no assurance that they are representative in character. The limitations of the reported data become all the more evident when it is recalled that they were collected long before the present improvement in agriculture. What it would be interesting to know is how far calorie needs are met *today* when for most of the developing regions calorie supplies *per caput* are within a few points of the average needs or, as in the case of Latin America, even in excess of them. Clearly we face here the problem of describing and measuring distributions of the main mass of lower intakes so that we may estimate the incidence of undernutrition for given levels of calorie availability and known values of variability in intake. The task is too big to be attempted. I can, however, suggest a possible formula.

The negative exponential has been used to describe and measure the lower mass of incomes and data for Maharashtra fit well with the description. Since the main cause of variation in calorie intake is inadequate income to purchase the diet, and since a major part of the income at the lower strata is spent on food, it would appear that the same form of distribution should fit the intake data equally well. We find this to be the case though, as Clark observes, the fit becomes less and less satisfactory at the upper range of the distribution. With the upper range however we are not concerned here.

The distribution function for a variable x distributed according to a negative exponential is given by

$$F(x) = 1 - e^{-\frac{x-b}{\sigma}}$$

with b representing the minimum intake compatible with survival and σ representing the standard deviation of the distribution given by the difference between the mean intake and the minimum, i.e. $\bar{x}-b$.

For a healthy active population of adults of the "reference" type in a developing country, with no one undernourished, the intake x will always exceed the calories needed for maintenance i.e. C_m so that we have:

$b=C_m$

$\sigma=$ average requirement of the adult man of reference type $-C_m$

$\quad=2,700-1,900$

$\quad=800$

and $F(x_{\min})=0$.

Ordinarily, b will be less than C_m but always higher than the calories needed for basal metabolism say C_B. Likewise σ will vary from $\bar{x}-C_m$ to $\bar{x}-C_B$. Clearly as b will increase, σ will decrease. The determination of b for any situation has to be empirical. When $\bar{x}$ is equal to the average requirement σ will vary over the range 800 to 1,400.

For any given value of b and σ the incidence of undernutrition will be:

$$I=1-e^{-\frac{Cm-b}{\sigma}}, \qquad \text{where } \sigma=\bar{x}-b.$$

In Table VII we have given values of the expected incidence for different values of calorie supply available for consumption per nutrition unit $\bar{x}$ and the standard deviation σ. It will be seen that when the supply per nutrition unit is about 2,400 calories, as was the case for India around 1965, nearly 40 per cent of the people failed to meet the needs, i.e. were undernourished. Today the current level of supply is about 2,500 to 2,600 calories per nutrition unit. Assuming that σ remained unchanged at the level of 1965, we can place the incidence between 25 and 33 per cent. As supply level improves to meet the needs, as one hopes would happen with the progress of programmes for raising the high-yielding varieties, we may expect further reduction in the incidence of undernutrition. But even when the supply is equal to the needs the incidence will continue to be of the order of 20 per cent assuming that σ will not have increased in the meanwhile. If σ tends to increase with the increase in the supply *per caput* as one would expect under the model we have assumed, the incidence of under-nutrition will be higher than 20 per cent. We must therefore stress the need to ensure that the inequalities in calorie intake do not increase further and indeed one hopes that a determined effort is made to reduce them. With the rich pressing for dietary variety, the supply to meet the energy needs based on cereals becomes increasingly oriented to the demand for expensive foods; hence it is likely to prove inadequate in holding down inequalities in calorie intake. With the constraint on supply of cereals removed, the issue before the countries today is primarily one of reducing inequalities in calorie intake by raising income levels of the poor, while simultaneously ensuring that the supply level is firmly held at or above the average needs—at prices within the reach of the poor. To put it differently the issue is how to generate income growth and yet produce income among the poor sufficient for them to buy adequate diet. Further discussion of Table VII is beyond the scope of this paper.

TABLE VII

Predicted prevalence of undernutrition for different levels of calorie per caput x̄ and standard deviation σ

x̄ \ σ	800	1,000	1,200	1,400
2,400	·32	·39		
2,500	·22	·33	·39	
2,600	·11	·26	·34	
2,700		·18	·28	·35

It would be too bold to generalize a conclusion regarding the extent of hunger on the basis of the data for a part of India. As we saw, in 3 of the 4 developing regions the calorie intake is within 5 to 7 per cent of the average needs and can therefore be taken to be of the order of 2,500 to 2,600 calories per nutrition unit. At these levels of intake, assuming that the standard deviation remains unchanged at the level in Maharashtra, about a quarter to one third of the people can be considered to be undernourished.

Protein Malnutrition

The same formula can also be used for estimating the incidence of protein malnutrition. It is not enough to consider the distribution of protein intake alone, however, because the utilization of protein in the diet depends on whether the calorie level is adequate or not. Diets must therefore be examined simultaneously for protein and calorie intake. Given such bivariate data an estimate of the incidence of protein deficiency would be

$$I=A+B+E$$

where A, B and E denote the frequencies in the cells of the figure shown below:

Protein

	A	B
Calories
	E	F

in which the dividing lines are placed at the critical limits for calories and protein given by the average requirement of the nutrition unit minus λ times the standard deviation.

The critical limits are set so low that the probability of individuals of the reference type having lower physiological requirements is very small. As I have said, it is because the critical limit for calories happens to be about the same as the calories needed for maintenance of nitrogen balance in adults that the expression given above provides us with an estimate of the total incidence of protein deficiency whether due to lack of adequate protein in the diet, or due to lack of adequate calories, or both.

Table VIII analyses the results of dietary surveys conducted in India (Sukhatme, 1970). It will be seen that most households which are protein deficient are also calorie deficient. Further, an appreciable proportion of the households although receiving adequate protein, suffer from inadequate calorie supply. Only about 5 per cent of the total diets seem to be deficient in protein *per se*. The analyses confirm the crucial importance of increasing diets to provide adequate calories for the solution of the protein problem. It is in the section of the population whose diet is deficient both in proteins and calories, or whose protein intake though adequate is not fully utilized for lack of adequate calories, that the main incidence of protein malnutrition occurs.

It follows that energy and not protein is the limiting factor in the diets of the people. We do not have bivariate data, of the type shown in Table VIII, for other countries. But there is ample evidence to show that where, as in India, the staple food is a cereal—rice, wheat etc.—and is accompanied by minimal quantities of pulses and vegetables, as appears to be the case in most countries of Asia and Latin America, the protein-calorie concentration of diets will be adequate to meet the protein needs provided the diet is taken in quantity adequate to meet energy needs (Gopalan, 1968). Diets heavily dependent upon starchy roots, sugar, or fat are exceptions but such cases appear too few to justify emphasis on increasing the supply of protein *per se* rather than on creating effective demand among the poor to enable them to buy adequate food.

TABLE VIII

Per cent incidence of protein and calorie deficiency (PD and CD) in four states of India: Andhra, Bihar, Madras and Maharashtra

| | *Andhra based on 2,675 Households* | | | | *Bihar based on 2,474 Households* | | |
	PD	NPD	Sub-Total		PD	NPD	Sub-Total
CD	14	12	26	CD	5	12	17
	(4·8)	(6·0)			(6·0)	(7·6)	
NCD	6	68	74	NCD	—	83	83
	(4·2)	(5·5)			(4·4)	(6·8)	
Sub-Total	20	80	100	Sub-Total	5	95	100

| | *Madras based on 1,022 Households* | | | | *Maharashtra based on 862 Households* | | |
	PD	NPD	Sub-Total		PD	NPD	Sub-Total
CD	28	21	49	CD	23	9	32
	(4·8)	(6·8)			(5·1)	(6·8)	
NCD	6	45	51	NCD	5	63	68
	(4·0)	(5·6)			(3·1)	(5·7)	
Sub-Total	34	66	100	Sub-Total	28	72	100

CD(Calorie Deficient) and NCD(Not Calorie Deficient), % households with daily calorie per nutrition unit below and above 2,200 Kcal respectively.

PD(Protein Deficient) and NPD(Not Protein Deficient), % households with daily protein per nutrition unit below and above 27g respectively.

Figures in parentheses are mean % of the household diets.

To summarize, between a quarter to one-third of the people in the developing countries do not get enough to eat to satisfy their calorie needs, a slightly larger proportion do not satisfy their protein needs for health; almost all the people who do not satisfy their protein needs do not satisfy their calorie needs either; and the proportion of people who do not have enough protein only is very small. In other words there is no evidence in the developing countries that the quality and concentration of protein in the diets commonly eaten, provided the quantity is enough to provide the necessary energy, is inadequate to meet protein needs for health.

Conclusion

Why, one may ask, have earlier studies reached such different conclusions? The main reason is that by examining the diets simultaneously for the two variates the interrelationship between protein and calories had now been taken into account. The other reason briefly, can be traced to the difference in interpretation placed on the meaning of requirement in the study of intake distributions. I conclude by quoting from a recent article by the late Sir Norman Wright:

> I well remember the occasion, when that distinguished statistician Sir Arthur Bowley, noting that the mean level of calories consumed by the British population in the Spartan period of the early post-war years coincided almost exactly with the accepted calorie requirements concluded (to the consternation of officials in the Ministry concerned) that some 50 per cent of the population must be undernourished. His argument was that if intake x, and requirement y are each normally distributed with the same mean, then the difference can be considered to be normally distributed around zero with a given standard deviation. It followed that the probability of y exceeding x or that a person is undernourished is $1/2$.

In reproducing the quotation above, it is not my intention to criticize the late Sir Arthur Bowley for a pronouncement which he may have made but which to the best of my knowledge he never published. There is nothing surprising either if the officials of the Ministry concerned were taken aback by his assessment. The suggestion that half the people of U.K. were either losing body weight, or were forced to reduce their physical activity for want of adequate food, or both, would always have serious policy implications which no Government would accept without having factual data to support it. This was fifty years ago. The fact of the matter is that the concept of requirement had not been fully developed at that time, and certainly not to the stage which could permit assessment of the type we are asked to make to-day for the developing countries. The point of quoting Bowley's assessment is to suggest that apparently we are confronted to-day with much the same argument that he then put forward, though in a new form and under more sophisticated mathematical formulation.

References

Edholm, O. G., Adam, J. M., Healy, M. J. R., Wolff, H. S., Goldsmith, R. and Best, T. W. (1970). Food intake and energy expenditure of army recruits. *Br. J. Nutr.* **24,** 1091.

Edholm, O. G., Fletcher, J. G., Widdowson, E. M. and McCance, R. A. (1955). The energy expenditure and food intake of individual men. *Br. J. Nutr.* **9,** 286.

FAO. (1957a). *Calorie Requirements*. Report No. 15. Rome: FAO.

FAO. (1957b). *Protein Requirements*. Report No. 16. Rome: FAO.

FAO. (1971). *Commodity Projections 1970–80*. Rome: FAO.

FAO/WHO. (1965). *Protein Requirements*. Nutrition Meeting Report Series No. 37. Rome: FAO.

FAO/WHO. (1970). *Expert Committee on Nutrition. Eighth Report*. p. 29. Geneva: WHO.

FAO/WHO. (1971). *Report of the Joint FAO/WHO Committee of Experts on Requirements for Protein and Energy*. (In press).

Gopalan, C. (1968). *Calorie Deficiencies and Protein Deficiencies*. Edited by R. A. McCance and E. M. Widdowson. London: Churchill.

Harries, J. M., Hobson, E. A. and Hollingsworth, D. F. (1961). Variations in energy expenditure and intake. *Bull. Inst. Stat.* **39**, *4*, 3.

Indian Council for Medical Research. (1968). *Recommended Dietary Allowances for Indians*. Delhi: Indian Council of Medical Research.

Sukhatme, P. V. (1961). The world's hunger and future needs in food supplies. *J. R. statist. Soc.* **124,** 463.

Sukhatme, P. V. (1966). The world's food supplies. *J. R. statist. Soc.* **129,** 222.

Sukhatme, P. V. (1970). Incidence of protein deficiency in relation to different diets in India. *Br. J. Nutr.* **24,** 477.

United Nations. (1968). *International Action to Avert the Impending Protein Crisis*. Report to the Economic and Social Council. New York: United Nations.

Adverse Effect of Sickness on Tropical Agriculture

MARGARET HASWELL

*Institute of Agricultural Economics, University of Oxford, and
Queen Elizabeth House, Oxford, England*

Preventive measures cost money
Curative measures mean money

Among the most exploited epithets of our times are "surplus labour" and "misery belts": as one man falls out another takes his place, but the level of productivity remains at the "poverty line". In examining concepts on surplus labour in under-developed agricultural economies, Cho (1963) reproaches the economists who talk about "human investment" in terms of education when human investment in terms of health seems more urgent.

At the *macro*-level, if cholera for example hits coal mining, its economic effects can be readily quantified in terms of so many millions of tons lost, and steps can be taken to prevent its recurrence. But the *micro*-level effects of sickness are appallingly neglected; for example, tuberculosis will be at a fully advanced stage at the peak of a man's economic activity, and when this strikes the head of a rural household there are serious economic effects caused by the loss of this man. To declare the problem requires a set of measurements from which it will be possible to correlate labour input with health status—a problem which is not simply a question of seasonal factors, but that the small man cannot afford to be sick while the bigger man can hire labour and get medical treatment. Meanwhile, the technologists continue to call for increased output from agriculture through diversification and intensification programmes, but the cultivator who is dependent primarily on family labour remains largely unwilling to exchange time-honoured methods for new productivity-raising methods which demand *greater human effort*.

45

The Constraint of Rural "Isolation"

The hypothesis presented here is that this resistance has its roots in the health status of rural communities in tropical countries with over-whelmingly large rural sectors, wherever people are isolated from the urban and administrative centres by lack of any modern means of transport. Distance is a critical determinant of medical care; this paper sets out to examine the effect of this factor on an agriculture which relies upon a labour force which is subject to a high incidence of fall-out from acute sickness, or is operating at low levels of productivity because it is carrying a significant proportion of the chronically sick. This approach will be reinforced by reference to the important contribution by Diesfeld of the Institut für Tropenhygiene und Öffentliches Gesundheitswesen am Südasien-Institut der Universität Heidelberg, who has applied the "theory of central places" to an analysis of hospital services using the criteria of attractivity and accessibility.*

Traditional agricultural practice involves a number of operations which require different intensities of energy output or work; and for certain operations cultivators are inclined to rest a great deal, as well as depending on division of labour between the sexes and by age groups to carry them through the agricultural cycle of activity. In a short wet, single crop, long dry season situation, concentration of labour on agricultural operations will be confined to little more than half the year, but the debilitating effects of chronic disease lead not only to pre-occupation with planting simply to meet home consumption needs, but also to delayed planting which reduces yields.

The main causes of dry season health hazards are lack of water, drinking "dirty" water, and dust; and diseases of the upper respiratory tract remain prevalent during the wet season which coincides with the heaviest period of agricultural work. Such regions, by definition, are invariably remote from sizeable urban areas, are served by poor road conditions, and are characterized by a significantly lower dependency ratio than is generally found in areas of relatively good road networks, water supply, and accessibility to an urban centre. The participation, or activity rate, is one of the most critical factors in arriving at some measure of production loss through chronic and acute sickness. In poorer, more remote, areas the dependency ratio is frequently rather less than 2:1, whereas in easily accessible areas it is more often of the order of 3:1. To some extent, the higher dependency ratio of urban-oriented farm family households may be correlated with higher survival

---

* Originally introduced by Christaller who estimated the central function of a place by counting the number of telephone connections.

rates of children. For example, it has recently been reported in North-East Thailand that rural children are "falling victim to a strange disease" which induces sudden coma and early death. The disease, known as Reye's syndrome* after it was first described by Doctor Reye of Australia in 1963, was "discovered" in Thailand by the SEATO Medical Research Laboratory in 1968.

The climate of this region in South-East Asia is tropical with temperatures rarely falling below 18°C (64°F) and with almost all the rainfall occurring with the south-west Monsoon from April to September. Olson *et al.* (1971) draw attention to the fact that:

> during the dry season the land is arid and water is in short supply. The highest temperatures, 37° to 41°C (98° to 106°F) occur during March and April, and during this time diarrhoeal disorders are common, much of it presumably due to water-born pathogens. Drinking water sources mainly include impoundment reservoirs or shallow dug wells . . . the rural people rarely consult a physician for trivial illnesses so that in many instances conditions are far advanced before being seen by a trained medical practitioner.

The number of improved roads is limited so that:

> travel of only a few kilometres may be difficult. During the rainy season travel in many areas is impossible because of flooding: in these instances many villages become completely isolated.

The physical findings of the children admitted to Udorn Hospital in the North-East showed that all appeared to be "well nourished"; investigators observed that:

> almost all patients were from rural areas and were between one and six years of age. The disease is characterized by the abrupt onset of central nervous system symptoms, and 70 per cent of the patients pursue a rapidly fatal course.

Although incidence of this disease, which is essentially a disease of children, does not have an obviously direct effect on tropical agriculture that can be measured in terms of loss of output, it is significant that the investigators conclude that:

> the apparent tendency of cases to originate from villages close to improved roads presumably indicates the importance of rapid transportation as a determinant in presenting to the hospital. Due to the extremely rapid course of this disease, many children undoubtedly die of this disorder before reaching the hospital. This was confirmed by a survey of 21 remote

---

* Huttenlocher reports that over the past several years Reye's syndrome has become widely recognized as a distinct clinical and pathologic entity. The relationship of this disorder to a variety of viral illnesses, including influenza B and A and varicella, has been well documented, but the exact cause of the hepatic and cerebral dysfunction remains obscure.

villages . . . Only about 10 per cent had reached the hospital before dying . . . The lack of improved roads, the peak occurrence of this syndrome towards the end of the rainy season when travelling is difficult, and the rapidity of death after the onset of symptoms, undoubtedly mean that the incidence of this disease is even greater than is apparent from hospital records.

Such occurrences pose the question as to whether natural increase is possibly being surpassed by infant and child mortality in many of the more remote tropical regions. Certainly the heavy dependence on family labour for the production of subsistence needs places special emphasis on the degree of adult female participation, and that of members of the older age groups of both male and female children.

The Diesfeld Concept for the Evaluation of Hospital Services

Diesfeld (1970) introduces a new concept for the evaluation of hospital services in developing countries, based on data from health reports of 50 hospitals in East Africa, in which he defines the hospital catchment area and its population as the denominator needed for comparability. He observes that:

> up to a certain distance from the hospital the assumption of equal chance might be true, particularly since hospitals usually are situated at admini- strative centres which provide in addition other public services and market facilities attracting people. But, for a more refined analysis of the population of a catchment area the functional interactions between the hospital and its surroundings have to be considered—shortly, the attract- ivity of the hospital.

An important factor relating to his second criterion—accessibility—he states to be (see Table I):

> the distance from the next hospital . . . Furthermore, the topographic situation of the hospital (in a valley, on a slope, or on the top of a hill) as well as the travel conditions during the wet season are of importance.

Diesfeld quotes surveys of Fendall (1963) and King (1966) as having shown for East Africa:

> that people are prepared to walk up to 10 miles (16 km) if transport is not available, and King (1966) was able to demonstrate that the average annual number of out-patient attendances dropped exponentially with the distance of the patient's home. If one takes into consideration the increasing importance of public and private transport which already opens up remote areas, the radius can be enlarged . . . But the maximum distance patients are prepared to travel varies with the severity of the disease and other factors.

TABLE I
Criteria used to evaluate hospital services

P1 = *Attractivity:*
  Hospital type
  No. of beds
  Diagnosis facilities
  No. of medical doctors
  No. of medical personnel
P2 = *Accessibility:*
  No. of health centres
  Distance from hospital of higher priority
  Type of administrative centre
  Road network
  Topographic situation
P3 = *Catchment area:*
  Population (1965)
  Catchment area (km²)
  Population density/km²

The "hospital recording rate" is the observed number of each diagnosis in a given period of time, divided by the "effective population" of the "hospital catchment area". The "hospital catchment area" and the "effective population" are defined by scores reflecting the estimated "degree of centrality", which is considering the attractivity and accessibility of the single hospital and the demographic situation in the hospital area.

Source: Diesfeld, (1970).

Diesfeld (1972) describes the theoretical catchment area of a hospital as an area with an intermediate radius of 15 km, maximum walking distance (Zone 1), a middle radius of 30 km (Zone 2), and an extended radius of 45 km (Zone 3); the model of a catchment area he modified however by the determinants: over-lapping catchment areas of neighbouring hospitals, natural boundaries crossing the catchment area, demographic factors, and attractivity and accessibility of the hospital in relation to neighbouring hospitals (Table I).

Of the 50 East-African hospitals listed in Diesfeld's theoretical model to evaluate hospital services according to the two criteria attractivity and accessibility and weighted by a scoring system, the twelve located in Uganda offer a useful illustration for the purpose of this paper (Fig. 1). Attractivity in relation to accessibility and catchment area (Table II) indicates that in three of these locations only—Jinja, Mbale, and Ngora—are the hospital infra-structural needs of the area met; Jinja and Mbale (together with Kampala and Tororo) are the areas in which urban development has concentrated, and which also support a relatively dense rural population with access to a favourable main road network (Fig. 1). Amudat on the other hand, is a relatively remote area served only by a small non-government hospital (Fig. 1), which meets neither the accessibility criterion, nor the requirement of the catchment area.

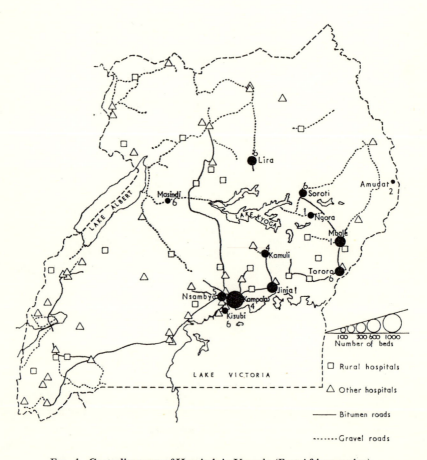

FIG. 1. Centrality score of Hospitals in Uganda (East African region).

Sources: **Location of twelve hospitals with place names after Diesfeld (1970); relevant roads, size of the twelve hospitals in terms of number of beds, and location of other hospitals in Uganda compiled from maps presented in** *Third Five-Year Development Plan, Uganda, 1971/2–1975/6.*

TABLE II

Attractivity in relation to accessibility and catchment area: 12 hospitals in Uganda of 50 listed in the East-African Region

Code No.	Hospital		Score*
1.	Jinja Mbale Ngora	$P1\begin{matrix}=P2\\=P3\end{matrix}$	Hospital size is in accordance with the accessibility factor, and in accordance with the catchment area, i.e. meets the hospital infrastructural needs of the area.
2.	Amudat	$P1\begin{matrix}=P2\\<P3\end{matrix}$	Hospital size is in accordance with the accessibility factor, but neither meet the requirement of the catchment area.
3.	—	$P1\begin{matrix}=P2\\>P3\end{matrix}$	Hospital size is in accordance with the accessibility factor, but the catchment area has a low density of population.
4.	Kampala Kamuli	$P1\begin{matrix}<P2\\=P3\end{matrix}$	Hospital size is adequate as far as population is concerned, but the criterion of accessibility is not satisfied.
5.	Nsambya	$P1\begin{matrix}>P2\\=P3\end{matrix}$	Accessibility is particularly good in relation to both the size of the hospital and the catchment area.
6.	Masindi Kisubi Tororo Soroti Lira	$P1\begin{matrix}<P2\\<P3\end{matrix}$	Hospital size is too small in terms of both accessibility and population.
7.	—	$P1\begin{matrix}>P2\\>P3\end{matrix}$	Hospital size is more than adequate in relation to both its accessibility and the population of the catchment area.
8.	—	$P1\begin{matrix}<P2\\>P3\end{matrix}$	There is an excess of hospital and accessibility services in relation to population density within the catchment area.
9.	—	$P1\begin{matrix}>P2\\<P3\end{matrix}$	Accessibility is more than adequate, but the hospital is too small to meet the needs of the population in the catchment area.

Sources: Diesfeld, (1970, 1972).

* For clarification, the full range of Diesfeld's score is presented; for evidence on the scores attained by the remaining 38 hospitals (35 in Kenya and 3 in Tanzania) in his sample of 50 the source material should be consulted.

Has Bergman an important lesson to impart when, in re-examining health manpower, he claims that:

the quest for power and control by professional groups and its economic accompaniment is unrelenting,

and that:

there continues an inability to focus on the health needs of people and last on self-interest?

Weitz (1971) reiterates:

To raise the standard of services in the rural areas, qualified manpower is needed to operate them, but such people are unwilling to live in the villages precisely because of the low level of services found there.

Water and Health are Intimately Interwoven with Economic Progress

Surtees points out:

Together with wheat, rice forms the staple diet of about 80 per cent of the world's population. In 1965, 300 million acres (120 million hectares) were under rice cultivation, comparedwi th 530 million (212 million hectares) of wheat, and 245 million (98 million hectares) of maize. Between 1958 and 1965, rice production increased by about 25 per cent due mainly to a further 17 million acres (6·8 million hectares) being developed.

Surtees is concerned about mosquitoes breeding in rice fields, and he stresses that the:

first most important step in reducing the hazard to man's health must be taken at the planning stage . . . Above all, it must be recognised that it is uneconomic to grow a crop which results in a reduced standard of health of workers involved.

Table III gives an indication of the economic cost of ill health from attacks of malaria as it affects small-scale producers on Colonization Schemes in the Dry Zone of Ceylon (which are fully irrigated for the production of rice and other subsistence crops).

Footnotes to Table III, p. 53 Activity threatened:

Case No. 1. First weeding of cotton crop. Income from this needed for essential food purchases.

Case No. 2. Sim-sim harvest; no labour available for hiring, pods cracked and harvest lost.

Case No. 3. Production of the staple foodgrain for home consumption.

Case No. 4. Production of the staple foodgrain for home consumption.

Case No. 5. Planting of staple foodgrain; wife obtained assistance with part of holding but insufficient labour available to plant up the whole area.

Case No. 6. Production of staple foodgrain for home consumption; sub-let holding for half-share of gross output, but saved hired labour component of his normal practice; by sub-letting therefore he reduced subsistence production foregone through sickness to a minimum.

TABLE III

*Some costs of ill-health to small-scale farmers who rely principally on family labour for subsistence production**

Case No.	Sickness/Injury	Age	Sex	Cost of hiring labour arising from sickness	Costs of inputs forfeited through sickness					Person† years of family subsistence foregone
					Seed	Manual labour	Animal labour	Loss of output	Total	
Uganda					*kg. millet equivalent*					
1	*Injured hand:* admitted to hospital for wound to be lanced, and subsequently treated as out-patient for periodic dressings, a distance of 17·6 km. walking	50	M	33	—	—	—	—	33	0·11
2	*Miscarriage:* possibly induced	30	F	—	5	90	20	111	226	0·75
Philippines					*kg. paddy equivalent*					
3	*Kidney complaint:* admitted to hospital and bed-ridden for three months	45	M	308	—	—	—	—	308	1·03
4	*Pulmonary tuberculosis:* badly needs money for treatment	62	M	780	—	—	—	—	780	2·60
Ceylon										
5	*Malaria:* developed high fever	34	M	297	—	—	—	417	714	2·38
6	*Malaria and chest complaint:* admitted to hospital	43	M	—	—	—	—	121	121	0·40

* Calculated from data collected for Uganda by D. K. Honeybone, The Philippines by J. C. Macalindong, and Ceylon by G. M. Abayaratna, all of whom were under the general direction of the writer at the time of the investigation.
† 300 kg grain equivalent per person per year taken as the subsistence minimum.

It was the *point in time* at which Case 5 fell sick with malaria that was particularly vulnerable; this was just at the beginning of the planting season and he was not fit again until well into the harvest. This man has four very young children to support whose wife could not manage alone. Had he been fully fit to work throughout the agricultural year, the return to family labour in that year would have been of the order of 2,000 kg paddy—and it would not have been necessary to expend some 300 kg paddy equivalent* on hired labour.

Although Case 6 appears to have been less severely hit economically, he had six young children and a wife to support and as his illness became more and more prolonged he was finally forced to borrow 700 kg of paddy to feed his family; this he obtained from a local middleman at a high interest rate. Malaria, which remains prevalent in irrigated resettlement areas, is caused to a large extent by bad drainage, uncleared weeds lining irrigation channels, and the mini-altitude levels of inadequate levelling of land prior to irrigation which encourages isolated pools which support developing larvae.

Tuberculosis is referred to by Banks (1969) as the "captain of the men of death" in present-day low income tropical countries. Fendall (1967) gives estimates of the number of people infected every year in East Africa alone: the disease develops in 60,000, diagnosis is made in 20,000, but successful treatment is given to only 10,000. Pulmonary tuberculosis is frequently contracted through inhaling dust which contains the tubercle bacilli. The bacilli can live for months in dust so that they are a constant source of danger. Spitting is a universal habit and infected persons cause rapid spread of the disease; low resistance may be associated with co-existence of malarial and parasitic infections. The chronic condition often referred to in tuberculosis as "modified" is so only in the sense that it is modified by primary infection. In hot countries which suffer long dry seasons, where various types of transport ply to and fro on *dusty unsurfaced* roads covering both man and vegetation alike with thick layers of yellow sand as they pass, inhalation through the respiratory tract is virtually unavoidable.

Case 4 is that of a man at an acute stage and in need of prolonged hospital treatment; but he lacks the means, is already burdened by debt, and in desperation has resorted to gambling. Case 3, on the other

---

* Clark and Haswell (1970) employ the de Vries generalization about the early stages of agricultural progress in which all measurements are made in kg of unmilled grain equivalent/total population/year; according to this generalization the true subsistence minimum stands at a little below 300 kg grain equivalent/person/year. Payments made to hired labour are usually in grain and where this is not so, money wages have been converted into grain equivalents, as also have other products, at the rate at which they exchange against grain in local markets.

hand, a farmer known to be hard working and to have made savings, was able to receive treatment in hospital; but this cost him all his savings. He had five very young children, and he was only able to hire labour sufficient for a small amount of food to be produced for his family. After he recovered, with the help of hired labour and a tractor, he was able to bring his farm back into full production, but during this period he was forced to borrow for food.

Fatigue, weakness, and weight loss, caused by water depletion in a man living in a hot climate is a much neglected aspect of health by technologists introducing programmes for increased output from agriculture; heat exhaustion and water debt severely limit the energy output of agricultural workers:

> Fresh water is essential for life . . . The average amount of water required daily for drinking, cooking, and washing is about 45 litres (10 gallons) per person, but considerably more than this is desirable, and in towns with piped water supplies and water carriage, sanitation consumption may average more than 200 litres (45 gallons) per person per day . . . By far the greater part of the population of the tropics lives in the rural areas where living conditions are extremely primitive . . . Water is obtained from highly polluted sources such as swamps, rivers, water holes, or unprotected wells, and is stored in and about houses in containers which breed mosquitoes; the surroundings of houses are littered with domestic refuse and the soil is contaminated by indiscriminate defaecation.

(Davey and Wilson, 1971).

Schram (1971) draws attention to the problem of water supplies and sewage disposal facing Nigeria after the war:

> For many towns piped and purified water was still a great luxury. The sources remained in large measure polluted rivers, swamps, and shallow contaminated wells. The larger towns had piped water often adequately treated but in inadequate amounts.
>
> Even in the capital, only 23 gallons per head was available in 1955;

and Schram observes that in Ibadan the supply was a mere 4 gallons per head.

The findings of a socio-economic survey of 244 households in the Agusan resettlement area of Mindanao, Southern Philippines, in 1969 (Anon, 1971) were that an alarming number of rural people rely on herbalists, "quack" doctors, and parents, and that health care facilities and services are a top priority. Ninety-six per cent of the population obtain their drinking water from open wells and other sources which are subject to contamination; and toilets are not yet recognised as a need of every home. During the period of the survey 13 per cent of the survey population were reported to have died. The most common causes of

c

death were high fever, dysentery, el tor cholera, broncho-pneumonia, malaria, miscarriage and premature delivery.

The level of living in the region is near the minimum for subsistence and:

> most of the resources have to be used for the pressing day-to-day need for food. Health and education of the people have very little claim on the limited resources of the community.

It is significant that in ranking priority needs, the first is for access roads, the second for land surveys and levelling for improved crop yields and increased agricultural output, and the third for safe drinking water and health care. All other facilities—irrigation, schools, markets, for example—are ranked as being of little use unless these three of highest priority are satisfactorily met.

References

Anon (1971). A Socio-Economic Survey of 244 Households in the Agusan Resettlement Area in 1969, *Committee on the Mindanao Agricultural Resettlement Agency Project*. Community Development Research Council, University of the Philippines.

Banks, A. L. (1969). Catastrophes and restraints. In *Population and Food Supply: Essays on Human Needs and Agricultural Prospects*. Edited by J. Hutchinson, London: Cambridge University Press.

Bergman, A. B. (1971). Health manpower re-examined. *Pediatrics J.*, **47** (6), 965–66.

Cho, Y. S. (1963) *"Disguised Unemployment" in Underdeveloped Areas: with special reference to South Korean Agriculture*. University of California Press.

Christaller, W. (1933). *Die zentralen Orte in Süddeutschland*.

Clark, C. and Haswell, M. (1970). *The Economics of Subsistence Agriculture*. London: Macmillian, 4th ed.

Davey, T. H. and Wilson, T. (1971). *The Control of Disease in the Tropics*. London: H. K. Lewis.

Diesfeld, H. J. (1970). The evaluation of hospital returns in developing countries. *Methods of Information in Medicine*, **9** (1), 27–34.

Diesfeld, H. J. (1972). Eine Methode zur Analyse der zentralörtlichen Bedeutung von Krankenhäusern als Grundlage der Krankenhaus-Regional-planung in Entwicklungsländern. *Der Krankenhausarzt*, **45** (4), 239–251.

Fendall, N. R. E. (1963). Health centres, a basis for a rural health service. *J. trop. Med. Hyg.*, **66**, 219–232.

Fendall, N. R. E. (1967). *Lancet* **II**, 1417.

Huttenlocher, P. R. (1972). Reye's syndrome: Relation of outcome to therapy, *Pediat. Pharmacol. Ther.*, **80** (5), 845–850.

King, J. (1966). *Medical Care in Developing Countries*. London: Oxford University Press.

Olson, L. C., Bourgeois, C. H., Cotton, R. B., Harikul, S., Grossman, R. A. and Smith, T. J. (1971). Reye's Syndrome, Toxic Encephalopathy Hypoglycemia, Fatty Liver, Aflatoxin. *Pediatrics J.*, **47** (4), 707–716.

Schram, R. (1971). *A History of the Nigerian Health Services*. Ibadan University Press.

Surtees, G. (1971). Control of mosquitoes breeding in rice fields. *J. trop. Med. Hyg.*, **74** (12), 255–259.

Weitz, R. (1971). *From Peasant to Farmer: A Revolutionary Strategy for Development.* New York and London: A Twentieth Century Fund Study. Columbia University Press.

Republic of Uganda. *Uganda's Third Five-Year Development Plan 1971/2–1975/6.*

The Energy Cost of "Food-Gathering"

J. H. LAWTON

Department of Biology, University of York, Heslington, York, England

Introduction

In thermodynamic terms, living organisms are open "steady state" systems, requiring a continual input of energy to maintain and structure their highly complex organization (Morowitz, 1968). All animals, including of course man, get the energy which they require from the food which they eat, and we can describe the utilization and transformation of the energy which animals eat by the following formulae:

$$C = P + R + F + U$$
$$A = C - F$$

where:

- C is the food energy consumed (eaten) per unit time by either an individual animal or a population;
- F is that part of the food energy that is not assimilated, and leaves the body as faeces;
- A is that part of the food energy that is taken into the body (absorbed or assimilated);
- P is that part of the absorbed energy that is incorporated (stored) as new animal tissue (production); it may appear as either growth of the individual or in the production of eggs and young;
- U is that part of the absorbed food energy that is eventually lost from the body as urine;
- R is that part of the absorbed food energy that is used in respiration and is eventually dissipated as heat. It is in this part of the energy budget that we are particularly interested in the present paper,

because it is in the process of respiration that living organisms make energy available to do the necessary work for the maintenance of their life-processes.

It will be seen that all the energy consumed is accounted for in these equations and that the first law of thermodynamics, which simply stated says that energy may be transformed from one form to another but cannot be created or destroyed, is therefore satisfied (Wiegert, 1968).

The basic unit of energy-budget measurements has been the calorie, the various terms in the above equations being quantified as calories per individual (or per unit of population) per unit time. More recently, energy-flows have been measured in joules. The interrelationship of these two units, together with several other useful units used in the paper, will be found in Appendix I.

The necessary work that living organisms must do to maintain and structure their complex organization is of many sorts; a great deal of the energy used in respiration, for example, is expended on "internal regulation"—that is in the sort of regulatory processes that are normally associated with classical whole animal and cellular physiology. But most animals must also move about, or at least maintain posture and position, and to maintain posture and move about against the forces of gravity and friction the animal must again do work and hence requires energy. This is also true of all the other many and varied tasks that animals perform on their environment, like drilling holes in trees, nest building or capturing prey. The proportion of assimilated energy (A) that animals use in respiration and hence in doing work is rather variable, but it is always fairly high. A colleague and I (McNeill and Lawton, 1970) have shown that, on average, for most poikilotherm populations ("cold-blooded" animals like insects, fish and snails) between 38 and 75 per cent of the energy assimilated is used in respiration, whilst in most homoiotherm populations ("warm-blooded" birds and mammals) the figure may be nearer 98 per cent.

We can now define the nature of our problem because the process of obtaining food (arguably the most basic of all the essential maintenance tasks, because without it none of the others are possible) itself requires work to be done and hence energy to be used; moving about to find food, obtaining it, processing it and eating it are all processes which require energy. For an animal to survive, therefore, it is obvious that the ratio:

Food energy absorbed (A)

Energy expended durings its collection

must be at least equal to one: preferably it should be much greater than one because the net surplus of energy generated must be used to drive all the remaining essential work-processes of the body. This problem has been dealt with theoretically by Schoener (1969), for a variety of predators, in an effort to understand the factors which control prey-selection. Details of this work need not concern us here, but it is obvious that theoretical studies of this type should be supported by adequate experimental data. At the present time, reliable studies on which the above ratio can be calculated are rather few, and an approximation to this ratio has been used in the present work, *viz*:

$$\frac{\text{Food energy gathered or consumed }(C)}{\text{Energy expended durings its collection}}.$$

Assuming that 50 per cent of the food eaten is actually assimilated (which is certainly true for the cases examined below) the minimum requirements for a viable feeding strategy are that this second ratio should not be less than 2. Using this second ratio, which we will call the ratio of energy gained to energy expended, the present paper examines the energy cost of obtaining food in a variety of animals (hummingbirds, a finch, a bumblebee, a damselfly larva, and a fish) and compares the results with similar information for "primitive" man and for certain aspects of modern high-intensity agriculture (cereal farming in Britain).

It should be noted that "food-gathering" has been used here in a very general sense to embrace both the process more correctly termed food-production by anthropologists (the cultivation of crops and their subsequent harvesting) and the process by which all animals and pre-agricultural man obtained their food and to which the term food-gathering in its strict sense is usually applied.

The "Food-gathering" Process

The energy costs associated with obtaining food can be summarized for convenience into six categories (Table I). Not all animals, of course, necessarily expend work in each category, and division into six separate items in no way implies that they are necessarily discrete in time and space during the food-gathering processes of a particular animal. Nevertheless, some such classification is a minimum first step given our present limited knowledge of the problem at least as far as most animals are concerned.

TABLE I

Summary of the main processes on which animals and man expend energy in "food-gathering"

Activity	Examples for animals other than man	Examples for man
i Energy cost of maintaining food supply	Small or non-existent: some exceptions e.g. ants which maintain aphid populations, and possibly part of the cost of territorial defence in some birds (Stiles, 1971) could be attributed to this category	Most (but not all) of the activities embraced by the word "farming" e.g. crop protection, animal husbandry, etc.
ii Energy cost of locating food supply	Probably of major importance in animals which have to hunt or forage for suitable food, and hence move about actively (Schmidt-Nielsen, 1972)	Non-existent in modern farming, but important in primitive man, as in hunting animals
iii Energy cost of gathering or catching food	Chasing, catching, overcoming and killing prey (Salt, 1967); energy used during grazing in herbivores (Golley and Buechner, 1968)	Harvesting in modern farming: very important
iv Energy cost of processing food	Probably very small for most animals; opening nuts in rodents (Rosenzweig and Sterner, 1970), cracking snails (thrush), or "chewing cud" (ruminants)	Very important, particularly in modern man, where food may be extensively processed before eating
v Energy cost of eating or swallowing food	Probably very small for most animals; may be important in species which swallow relatively large prey (Schoener, 1969); may be difficult to distinguish from iv	Small or negligible
vi Energy cost of transporting and storing food	Probably small for most animals; transport back to nest (bees, birds) or winter food-stores	Very important, particularly in modern man, where food may be transported long distances and stored for long periods

For most natural populations of animals, the energy costs of maintaining their food-supply (Category i) are included in the respiration of the organisms "supplying" the food (be it a plant or another animal) and are not attributable to the animals doing the collecting. In the case of the small number of animals (and in particular man) which actually expend energy themselves in maintaining their food-supplies, it is reasonable to assume that the maintenance costs of the "supplying" organism (plant or animal) should be correspondingly reduced, and this presumably leads to an increased productivity from the food-source (since energy not expended in respiration becomes available as production). This problem is discussed briefly for modern man by Odum (1971), but the energetics of such a system for a natural animal population (like aphid-tending ants) would repay detailed investigation.

It is obvious from Table I that the major expenditures of energy in food-gathering fall under very different categories for most animals compared with man. This will become clearer in the following examples.

The Energy Costs of Food-gathering in Various Animals

Table II summarizes the rather limited information that is available on the energy costs of food-gathering in five types of animal. The data are all taken from previously published studies which in three cases give sufficient information for the authors' own estimates of energy expended and gained during food-gathering to be used directly (Glass, 1971; Schartz and Zimmerman, 1971; Wolf and Hainsworth, 1971). The data show the maximum and minimum values for each species under the conditions specified in the original paper; these represent the total energies expended, and no attempt has been made to break them down into the various components listed in Table I.

In the remaining three cases, the data given by the authors were used to calculate the necessary figures, subject to a number of assumptions. In the case of the hummingbirds studied by Wolf et al. (1972), it was assumed that the birds spent between 2 and 10 seconds foraging per flower, and the figures shown are the best and worst performances from a total of three species feeding on three flower-types. These do not include the cost of flying between flowers, and because of this and because of the way in which they are calculated, must be regarded as only very approximate.

In the bumblebee *Bombus vagans* (Heinrich, 1972a) the energy costs of foraging were computed from estimates of the cost of flying between flowers, and the cost of maintaining a high thoracic temperature whilst

TABLE II

Summary of the energy costs of "food-gathering" in various animals

Animal	Author	Type of organism	Type of food and method of feeding	Absolute rate of energy expenditure in feeding (cal min^{-1})	Energy gained / Energy expended
Eugenes fulgenes	Wolf and Hainsworth (1971)	Tropical hummingbird	Rapid, hovering flight at experimental vials of sugar in the laboratory	32·9	7–70
Amazilia tzacatl Phaethornis superciliousus Thalurania furcata	Wolf, Hainsworth and Stiles (1972)	Three species of tropical hummingbird	Rapid, hovering flight at natural flowers in the field to collect nectar	16·1–21·5	3·8–22·2
Spiza americana	Schartz and Zimmerman (1971)	Dickcissel; a north American finch	Flitting through low vegetation in search of insects and seeds	15·6	12·8
Bombus vagans	Heinrich (1972a)	Bumblebee	Flight between *Epilobium* (fire weed) flowers for nectar; in cold weather, energy is also expended in maintaining a high thoracic temperature	0·32–0·46	4·4–20·2
Pyrrhosoma nymphula	Lawton (1971a)	Freshwater damselfly (Odonata) larva	Lying in wait for prey (other small aquatic insect larvae and crustacea) to swim past	5×10^{-5}– 5×10^{-6}	1·1–3·6
Micropterus salmoides	Glass (1971)	Largemouth black bass; freshwater fish	Swimming after small prey —fish (guppies) in the laboratory	2·2–3·0	3·8–10·3

the bees were actually on the flowers; this latter expenditure prevents the bees from becoming torpid and permits nectar collection to continue during cold weather. (It was found that estimates of the energy expended in "routine" metabolism were insignificant compared with the first two costs, and they have been omitted from the calculation.) The two values shown are those calculated for *B. vagans* at air temperatures of 10 and 24°C respectively. All the necessary information on the foraging behaviour at these two temperatures and the costs of maintaining a high thoracic temperature are given by Heinrich (1972a and b). Approximate flight-costs were estimated using Hocking's (1953) data on the energetics of flight in the hive-bee *Apis* which weighs slightly less than *Bombus vagans*; if anything this will underestimate the true foraging costs for *B. vagans*; nor have the costs of transport between the flowers and the nest been included.

The data on the damselfly larva *Pyrrhosoma nymphula* are from my own work (Lawton, 1971a), on the assumption that larvae (which lie in wait for prey and do not forage in the sense of actively looking for food) were essentially hunting the whole time. In the case of larvae in the field (from which these data are taken) this is almost certainly true, because at no time were they ever feeding close to their maximum daily rates (Lawton, 1971b), and larvae only refused food in the laboratory when they had been presented with far more food than they were ever likely to experience in the field. The figures shown in Table II were calculated from estimates of the energy expended in respiration per day and food-energy eaten per day, under the best and worst field-feeding conditions. The minimum ratio of energy gained to energy expended in *Pyrrhosoma* is very low (1·1); however, this is still, just, a viable food gathering strategy because of the very high efficiency with which food is assimilated in this species (Lawton, 1971c).

The most surprising thing about the data in Table II is the overall similarity in the ratio of energy gained to energy expended for the various species. This is true despite the fact that the absolute rates of energy expenditure during foraging vary over nearly eight orders of magnitude, from the very "high-cost" techniques of the hovering hummingbirds (with absolute rates of energy expenditure during foraging of between 16 and 33 cal min^{-1}) to the much lower values for *Micropterus* (2–3 cal min^{-1}) and *Bombus* (0·3–0·5 cal min^{-1}) and the extremely low values for the very inactive damselfly (5 × 10^{-5} to 5 × 10^{-6} cal min^{-1}). These differences are a result of both the sort of foraging behaviour used—flight is energetically much more expensive in terms of calories expended per unit time than sitting and waiting for prey to swim past and also the very different body-sizes of the animals in question. It is clear, however, that energetically expensive food-gathering techniques in animals can only be applied to food sources which guarantee a high rate of energy return, and this fact may be one of the reasons for the apparent convergence in the ratio of energy gained to energy expended for both the "high-cost" and "low-cost" strategies listed in Table II.

The similarity in the ratio of energy gained to energy expended is also surprising because of the large differences in the demands which the energy surplus generated in foraging must meet in the different species. These include all the requirements for physiological mainten-ance mentioned in the introduction, reproduction and growth, and any other activities carried out by the animal on its environment, excluding food-gathering. These demands are likely to be larger in larger animals and certainly larger in homoiotherms than poikilotherms. However, the simple ratio of energy gained to energy expended gives no indication of the total amount of net energy gained in feeding, which depends both on this ratio and the total amount of time spent feeding. An understanding of the sort of evolutionary forces operating on the food-gathering process might, therefore, be gained by asking how an animal could increase its net energy gain during feeding assuming that this is a desirable objective. There are three ways of doing this:

(a) to spend more time food-gathering at a more or less constant efficiency (i.e. constant ratio of energy gained to energy expen-ded). This is only a practical solution providing that the time required does not conflict with other essential activities like sleeping, courtship or avoiding predators. Our understanding of time-budgets in natural populations therefore becomes important in this respect (Stiles, 1971; Verner, 1965);

(b) to spend the same time food-gathering, but to increase the efficiency in some way; two possibilities are:

(i) to search or forage faster, thereby encountering more food per unit of time. However, the energy cost of moving about increases either in proportion to velocity (small mammals: Schmidt-Nielsen, 1972) or in some cases (e.g. fish) suprapro-portionally (Tytler, 1969), so that on energy considerations alone this may not be a viable solution; further work is required on the problem of what constitute, energetically, the most efficient searching rates in active food-gatherers;

(ii) to allocate the time spent foraging so that proportionally more is spent in areas of high food-energy availability; this approach seems to be the one adopted by some predators

(Schartz and Zimmerman, 1971; Smith and Dawkins, 1971) and has a number of important ecological consequences (Royama, 1971). Such a method, however, requires that areas of high feeding "profitability" are available, which is certainly not always the case.

There are, therefore, fairly severe restrictions on any of the solutions which animals might try, to increase their net gain of energy during food-gathering. It is clear also that precisely the same sort of restrictions will be operative for mankind.

The Energy Costs of "Food-gathering" in a Simple Human Society

Table III summarizes the energy costs of "food-gathering" for a human society operating in essentially the same way as in the five other types of animal discussed above.

TABLE III

Energy cost of "food-gathering" and food producing in a simple human society—Lamotrek Atoll in the Pacific; data from Odum (1971) after Alkire

Gains and expenditures	Kcal day^{-1}
Food eaten by population	0.59×10^6
Work done in:	
Tree harvesting—Coconuts and Breadfruit	0.007×10^6
Farming —Pigs and Taro	0.017×10^6
Fishing	0.008×10^6
Minor unquantified costs Fishing for turtles Collecting sea-urchins	?
Minimum total energy expended	0.032×10^6

$$\frac{\text{Energy gained}}{\text{Energy expended}} = \frac{0.59 \times 10^6}{0.032 \times 10^6} = 18.4$$

The food of the Lamotrek Atoll islanders consists of rootcrops (taro), coconuts and bread-fruit, with animal protein in the form of pigs, fish, turtles and sea-urchins. All the work in harvesting and catching their food is carried out entirely by human labour, and there is no external energy subsidy of any kind. The energy expended in obtaining food consists of both energy used to simply gather what is already there, and also energy expended in farming (i.e. producing and maintaining) a part of the food supply. The data shown in Table III are not complete, because the energy costs of gaining a number of minor components (turtles and sea-urchins) have not been estimated, but they are complete enough for our purposes. The most interesting thing from the point of view of an animal ecologist is the remarkable similarity between the ratio of energy gained to energy expended (18·4) in this simple human society, and the same ratio for the five types of animal listed in Table II.

The Energy Costs of "Food-gathering" in Modern Man (Cereal-farming in Britain)

A major factor in the evolution of a complex human society is the ability of a small number of individuals to supply the food requirements of a much larger number of people, who are then free to carry out a variety of tasks other than obtaining food, like art, mining, reading papers at conferences, or the manufacture of nuclear weapons. Essentially this means that the ratio of energy gained to human energy expended must be greatly increased. However, precisely the same limitations that were discussed above for animals also hold for man's capacity to increase his food-gathering efficiency, when he attempts to do this unaided. Primitive societies, unable to break out of these energetic restrictions must of necessity be unsophisticated with a large part of the population involved directly in food-production. The solution to this problem, on which the whole evolution of modern society is based, is to use some form of energy that is available to do work in food-producing and crop-maintenance in addition to the energy that is used directly by the human beings producing the food. Two low-intensity applications of this solution are to use either the energy supplied by water and wind, or to use animal labour (e.g. horses, cattle or camels), where the animals at least in part obtain their energy supply from a food-source that would not be used by man. This means that a part of the energy expended in obtaining food for human consumption does not have to be supplied by that food, with a consequent net gain of energy in human terms.

The high-intensity application of the solution is not to use animals or wind and water at all, but rather to use the energy supply available as fossil-fuel (coal, oil or gas) to do most of the work required in "food-gathering". The energy expended by the human beings involved in the operation then becomes very small and the net energy gained in terms of food produced relative to human energy expended large.

Although large numbers of us live on this basis at the present time, very few of us have any idea of the real energy costs of "food-gathering" in such a system. A tentative estimate of some of the basic costs are presented in Tables IV and V for a modern British cereal-farming system. Cereal farming has been chosen because this supplies us with a large part of our basic energy supply. Similar, though less precise, calculations for potatoes give essentially the same results, whilst inclusion of other vegetable foods and meat is unlikely to alter the substance of what follows, though it would certainly alter it in detail. In particular, the energy cost of producing meat using modern intensive techniques must be very large, simply because it involves energy expenditure at two levels rather than just one; that is in animal food-stuff production and animal husbandry.

TABLE IV

Summary of typical annual crop yields in British cereal-agriculture (see text for sources)

	Grain yields (*cwt per acre per annum*)		
	Low	Average	High
Winter wheat	28	33	38
Spring wheat	24	29	34
Barley	25	30	35
Oats	25	30	35
AVERAGE	25	30	35
	Grain yields (Kcal) *		
	Low	Average	High
per acre	4,657,000	5,588,500	6,519,900
per m²	1,151	1,381	1,611

* Assumes 15% moisture loss on harvested weight, and an energy value of 4,310 cal per g for unmilled grain.

TABLE V

Summary of typical energy costs involved in producing the crop-yields listed in Table IV (see text for sources); only primary costs are included, that is the energy actually used on the farm

Job	Hours per acre per annum	Gallons of diesel per acre p.a.	Kcal per acre per annum *
Fossil fuel costs			
Tractor**—	Premium 5	7·5	$31·4 \times 10^4$
tilling, sowing,	Average 8	12·0	$50·3 \times 10^4$
spraying, etc.			
Combine-harvester	0·3	0·5	$2·1 \times 10^4$
Grain-dryer	†	2·5–3·0	$10·5 \times 10^4$ to $12·6 \times 10^4$
TOTAL FOSSIL— FUEL COSTS	—	10·5–15·5	$44·0 \times 10^4$ to $64·9 \times 10^4$
Human labour costs			
Tractor driving	8	—	880‡
Combine-harvester and other misc. activities	2	—	220
TOTAL HUMAN LABOUR COSTS	—	—	1,100

* Diesel is $4·19 \times 10^4$ Kcal per gallon.

** Diesel consumption approx. 1·5 gallons per hour.

† Uses two gallons of diesel per ton of grain dried.

‡ 110 Kcal per hour for respiratory rate of reasonably active man.

The data shown in Tables IV and V are derived from a variety of sources. Information on crop yield, tractor and man-hours are from Nix (1969) supplemented by information from D. F. Lawton (personal communication). Energy values for cereals are from Cummins and Wuycheck (1971) and for diesel fuel from the Ministry of Power (1958). The respiratory energy costs of an "active" human-being, which are also involved in the calculations, will obviously vary markedly depending on what he is doing, as well as on environmental temperature. The figure used in Table V is an average value calculated from the resting metabolic rate of man (Prosser and Brown, 1961) by assuming that during the sort of activity involved (much of which consists of sitting driving machinery, but some, of course, involves very strenuous work) the respiratory rate will be approximately twice resting metabolism.

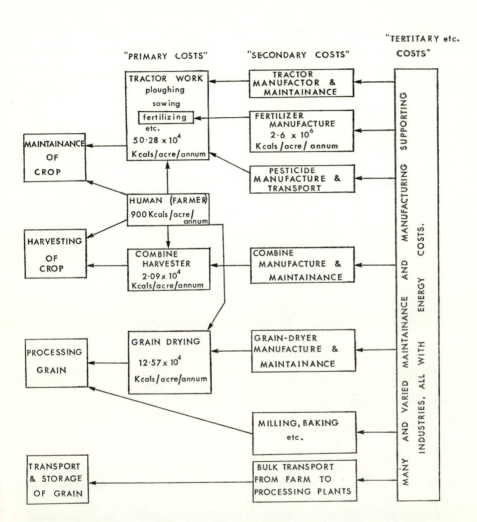

FIG. 1. A summary of the primary energy costs involved in a modern cereal-producing system, and their relationships to important secondary and tertiary energy costs; with one exception, only primary (i.e. on-farm) costs have been estimated.

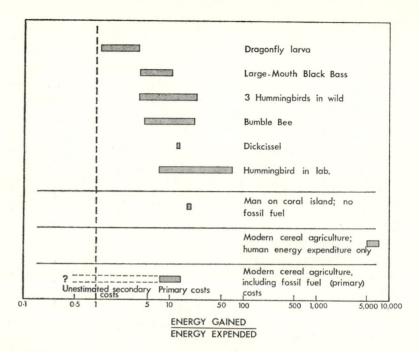

FIG. 2. A summary of the ratios of energy gained to energy expended in animals and man. Note that the scale is logarithmic.

A similar figure can be derived from more direct measurements of human energy consumption under a variety of activities and conditions (e.g. Banerjee and Saha, 1972; Gold *et al.*, 1969). The estimated energy costs of cereal production shown in Tables IV and V are the absolute minimum, or "primary costs" actually arising on the farm, and no attempt has been made to calculate the large energy costs involved in food processing and agricultural supporting industries (Fig. 1). Figure 2 makes an overall comparison between this agricultural system, and those discussed above.

The ratio of energy gained to energy expended in cereal farming, *taking into account just the energy used in human labour,* lies between 4,233 (4,657,000/1,100) and 5,926 (6,519,000/1,100) or approximately 4,000–6,000. This is some two or three orders of magnitude greater than in the more natural systems discussed previously, the very large net surplus of energy so generated being used to support members of the population who are not involved in "food-gathering". In England and Wales the ratio of the population directly employed in agriculture (farmers, farm workers and agricultural machinery drivers) to the total population is close to 1:75 (General Register Office, 1966) and although part of the population is obviously supported by imported food, it gives some idea of the efficiency with which modern farming techniques generate a large net-energy surplus. It would be fascinating to compare this ratio with comparable data on the food-gatherer: total population ratio in the social insect (bees, ants and termites), for which exactly the same principles hold (e.g. Wilson, 1968), but which do not have the benefit of an external energy source.

Whilst the net food energy yields in terms of human energy used to obtain the food are very large for a modern cereal farm the total energy costs, when diesel fuel consumption is included are much larger. Inclusion of fossil-fuel costs reduces the ratio of food energy gained to the total energy expended, to between 7 and 14, which is very similar to the sort of values shown for the other situations examined, although in this case the similarity is certainly misleading because unlike the other systems, only a fraction of the real energy costs have so far been included in the calculations in that no attempt has been made to work out the energy expended by the agricultural supporting industries, nor the energy costs associated with transporting, storing, and processing the food prior to consumption.

Some idea of how the estimate of energy consumption increases if these "secondary" and "tertiary" costs are included can be obtained by simply including the energy expended in the manufacture of nitrogen fertilizer. Assuming that an average cereal crop will receive approximately 1·5 cwt of N fertilizer per acre per annum (the actual figure is very variable; some like barley on rotation after sugar-beet may receive none), and since the energy cost of manufacturing synthetic nitrogen fertilizer can be as high as 35×10^6 Kcal per ton (G. Borgstrom, *in lit*) the cost of manufacturing the fertilizer used on the crop comes to an additional $2·6 \times 10^6$ Kcal per acre per annum. This alone is nearly half the energy yielded by the crop it is used to fertilize, and reduces the ratio of food energy gained to energy expended to between 1·4 and 2·1. Inclusion of other secondary and tertiary costs, which are as essential to this system as a beak is to a hummingbird will obviously reduce this ratio still further, and in all probability to considerably less than 1.

Conclusions

The ratio of energy gained to energy expended would appear to play a fundamental role in determing how an animal feeds, what it feeds on and what else it is able to do as well as feed. Because a self-supporting food-gathering strategy must always generate more energy than is expended during its collection, we expect and indeed we observe, that the food-gathering processes of most animals are very efficient.

There is little doubt that in most of our minds, we probably regard modern farming methods as being more efficient means of obtaining food than the methods employed by animals and primitive man; efficiency, however, depends entirely on your point of view, so that the criteria on which efficiencies are judged become important. More precisely, therefore, we may say that modern agricultural systems are extremely efficient at turning human effort into food, and moderately efficient, for example, at turning capital investment into profit. In terms of the ratio of human and fossil-fuel energy expenditure to total energy gain they are certainly no more efficient than the food-gathering systems of other animals and "primitive" man, and if the total energy expended in food processing and all the many and varied supporting industries are included, they are certainly considerably less efficient than most natural systems. Viewed against the food-gathering strategies of other animals and primitive man, modern man's undoubted success in providing more and more food with less and less labour for more and more mouths is seen as an energetic sleight-of-hand.

In terms of this symposium, the problem is very simple; the systems which we have devised to feed ourselves are energetically expensive, and rely completely on a readily available source of energy "external" to the energy expended by the human beings "guiding" the system. This is both a major factor permitting the existence of, as well as being necessitated by, our present high levels of population, organized into a complex, largely urban society remote from the sites where food is actually produced. How we will continue to operate this system of food-gathering when fossil-fuel is no longer so readily available, what alternative "high-energy" source will be available to take its place, and what sort of pollution and environmental problems these new sorts of energy for food-gathering will create are problems that we must urgently consider. One thing is clear: without continuous "high-energy" inputs into our agricultural system, we could neither continue to feed our present population, nor maintain the present organization of our society.

Acknowledgements

The calculations on modern cereal agriculture would not have been possible without the considerable help of my brother, David, who farms Hirdrifaig in North Wales; his knowledge of British agriculture was invaluable, although any errors in the calculations are my own! Dr. M. Macpherson gave me valuable help with data on diesel fuel, and several colleagues at York provided me with very valuable help and criticism during the preparation of this paper, in particular Professor J. D. Currey and Dr. M. J. Chadwick.

References

Banerjee, B. and Saha, N. (1972). Effect of temperature variation in a climatic chamber on energy cost of rest and work. *Env. Res.* **5,** 241–247.

Cummins, K. W. and Wuycheck, J. C. (1971). Caloric equivalents for investigations in ecological energetics. *Mitt. int. Ver. Limnol.* **18,** 1–158.

General Register Office (1966). *Census 1961 England and Wales Occupational Tables.* London: H.M.S.O.

Glass, N. R. (1971). Computer analysis of predation energetics in the large-mouth bass. In *Systems Analysis and Simulation in Ecology* Vol. 1. Edited by B. C. Patten. New York and London: Academic Press.

Gold, A. J., Zernitzer, A. and Samucloft, S. (1969). Influence of season and heat on energy expenditure during rest and exercise. *J. appl. Physiol.* **27,** 9–12.

Golley, F. B. and Buechner, H. K. (1968). *A Practical Guide to the Study of Productivity of Large Herbivores,* IBP Handbook No. 7. Oxford and Edinburgh: Blackwell.

Heinrich, B. (1972a). Temperature regulation in the bumblebee *Bombus vagans:* a field study. *Science* **175,** 185–187.

Heinrich, B. (1972b). Energetics of temperature regulation and foraging in a bumble-bee, *Bombus terricola* Kirby. *J. comp. Physiol.* **77,** 49–64.

Hocking, B. (1953). The intrinsic range and speed of flight of insects. *Trans. R. ent. Soc., London,* **104,** 223–347.

Lawton, J. H. (1971a). Ecological energetics studies on larvae of the damselfly *Pyrrhosoma nymphula* (Sulzer) (Odonata: Zygoptera). *J. Anim. Ecol.* **40,** 385–423.

Lawton, J. H. (1971b). Maximum and actual field feeding-rates in larvae of the damselfly *Pyrrhosoma nymphula* (Sulzer) (Odonata: Zygoptera). *Freshwat. Biol.* **1,** 99–111.

Lawton, J. H. (1971c). Feeding and food energy assimilation in larvae of the damsel-fly *Pyrrhosoma nymphula* (Sulzer) (Odonata: Zygoptera). *J. Anim. Ecol.* **39,** 669–89.

McNeill, S. and Lawton, J. H. (1970). Annual production and respiration in animal populations. *Nature, Lond.,* **225,** 472–474.

Ministry of Power (1958). *The Efficient Use of Fuel.* London: H.M.S.O.

Morowitz, H. J. (1968). *Energy Flow in Biology.* New York and London: Academic Press.

Nix, J. (1969). *Farm Management Pocketbook.* Ashford, Kent: Department of Agricultural Economics, Wye College.

Odum, H. T. (1971). *Environment, Power and Society.* New York, London: Wiley-Interscience.

Prosser, C. L. and Brown, F. A. (1961). *Comparative Animal Physiology.* Philadelphia and London: W. B. Saunders.

Rosenzweig, M. L. and Sterner, P. W. (1970). Population ecology of desert rodent communities: body size and seed-husking as bases for heteromyid coexistence. *Ecology,* **51,** 217–224.

Royama, T. (1971). Evolutionary significance of predators' response to local differences in prey density: a theoretical study. In *Dynamics of Populations*, Edited by P. J. den Boer and G. R. Gradwell, Wageningen: PUDOC.

Salt, G. W. (1967). Predation in an experimental protozoan population (*Woodruffia-Paramecium*). *Ecol. Monogr.*, **37**, 113–44.

Schartz, R. L. and Zimmerman, J. L. (1971). The time and energy budget of the male dickcissel (*Spiza americana*). *Condor*, **73**, 65–76.

Schmidt-Nielsen, K. (1972). Locomotion: energy cost of swimming, flying and running. *Science*, **177**, 222–228.

Schoener, T. W. (1969). Models of optimal size for solitary predators. *Amer. Nat.*, **103**, 277–313.

Smith, J. N. M. and Dawkins, R. (1971). The hunting behaviour of individual great tits in relation to spatial variations in their food density. *Anim. Behav.*, **19**, 695–706.

Stiles, F. G. (1971). Time, energy and territoriality of the anna hummingbird (*Calypte anna*). *Science*, **173**, 818–21.

Tytler, P. (1969). Relationship between oxygen consumption and swimming speed in the haddock, *Melanogrammus aeglefinus. Nature, Lond.*, **221**, 274–275.

Verner, J. A. (1965). Time budget of the male long-billed marsh wren during the breeding season. *Condor*, **67**, 125–139.

Wiegert, R. G. (1968). Thermodynamic considerations in animal nutrition. *Am. Zoologist*, **8**, 71–81.

Wilson, E. O. (1968). The ergonomics of caste in the social insects. *Amer. Nat.*, **102**, 41–66.

Wolf, L. L. and Hainsworth, F. R. (1971). Time and energy budgets of territorial hummingbirds. *Ecology*, **52**, 980–988.

Wolf, L. L., Hainsworth, F. R. and Stiles, F. G. (1972). Energetics of foraging: rate and efficiency of nectar extraction by hummingbirds. *Science*, **176**, 1351–1352.

Appendix I

Interrelationship of Units

1 calorie (cal) = 4·18 joules.

1 kilogram calorie (Kcal) = 1,000 calories.

1 acre = 4046·9 square meters (m²).

1 hectare = 10,000 m² = 2·47 acres.

1 hundredweight (cwt) = 0·05 tons = 50·8 kilograms.

Sources of Energy and Their Adequacy for Man's Needs

F. W. HUTBER

Department of Trade and Industry, London, England

C. I. K. FORSTER

Consultant, formerly of the Department of Trade and Industry, London, England

(The views expressed in this paper are the views of the authors and should not be taken to represent the views of the Department of Trade and Industry)

Everything in the universe, from the most complex compound, through the elements down to the particle of unit mass and beyond, is energy. Energy is indestructible and when it is changed from one perceivable form to another there is no loss. Thus, in one sense, there can be no question but that energy in its various sources is adequate to man's needs.

But so far the scientists of the world have succeeded in harnessing energy for everyday practical use from only relatively few sources. We therefore have to look at the main sources from which we now obtain energy, and any other potential sources from which we might obtain energy during the period of practical interest to us all.

We also have to consider the economics of various processes of production as the price at which energy can be made available is highly relevant, and we will also have to give some thought to the processes by which it is used, which themselves can be subject to change.

The main source of the energy we now use is the sun. Radiation energy (sunlight) falling on the earth is absorbed by it and mostly re-radiated out into space. The fraction of this energy retained is absorbed by vegetation and converted by photosynthesis into chemical energy which is essential for the life process. Most of the residues from the life process are oxidized by the atmosphere and lose their accessible chemical energy storage ability but some, by movement of the earth's crust causing the exclusion of oxygen and the passage of millions of years, resulted in the formation of the hydrocarbon fuels of coal, oil and natural gas which we diligently seek today. Such chemical fuels are clearly finite in extent and the marginal cost of finding and extracting them increases as the supplies become exhausted. The existence of the hydrocarbon fuels has been known to man for thousands of years but it is only in the last hundred years or so that the technology has become available to extract and use the energy usefully and cheaply, thus stimulating the demand for energy.

The second source we identify as originating in the "mechanics" of the world—tide, wind and water power. Each of these sources requires a rather restrictive set of physical conditions for extracting useful amounts of energy and is highly capital intensive, so that although operating costs are low, the resource requirements for construction are high and the physical limitations of siting etc. severely limit the amount of energy we can expect from the source.

The third source originates from the internal heat of the earth—a residue of its formation. In theory, this source is available all over the world but in practice exploitation has been limited to a few natural sites where the earth's crust is particularly thin thus reducing the capital cost of extraction very significantly.

The fourth source arises from the structure of matter itself. The "cement" of the atomic nucleus is energy and the rebuilding of the nucleus can be made to provide a surplus of energy. The nucleus of the heavy element uranium can readily be restructured in this way by the fission process but the amount of uranium found in the earth is finite and so therefore cannot be considered as an indefinitely ongoing source. Restructuring the other way by building heavier elements is possible using deuterium in the fusion process. Supplies of deuterium in the world are found in sea water and are therefore virtually boundless in extent; however, large amounts of energy are required to release energy in fusion and the technology is not yet available to do it, even on a laboratory scale.

We may think of energy as being of two kinds, primary energy and secondary energy. Coal (including lignite), oil and natural gas are the three main primary fuels of the day. Most electricity is produced from one or other of these primary fuels and so is regarded as secondary energy; but electricity can also be generated by water power, nuclear power and in some countries by geothermal power and we think of all these as primary electricity since, by and large, they are not in a usable form until converted into electricity. Other main secondary fuels include coke and other manufactured solid fuels together with the various types of gas made from coal or oil. Inevitably the fossil fuels cannot sustain indefinitely a demand for energy increasing at present rates. Either the rate of increase will have to be cut back and eventually demand be greatly reduced or other sources of primary energy will have to be developed. Of our main present day primary fuels only hydro-electricity and geothermal power are renewed year by year; their use will continue to expand but they cannot be expected to make up for a deficiency in other fuels. The arrival of nuclear fission power has extended the time limit before another substitute fuel becomes a necessity, but if it expands greatly in its present form the uranium available may not last long.

The potential imbalance between supply and demand increasing at present rates does not mean we are liable to wake up one morning and learn that there is an energy crisis. This can in fact happen at any time for short term reasons, whatever the underlying supply and demand position, but looked at in a longer term context what would happen would be determined by economics. As the world moved towards a shortage, energy prices would tend to rise—whether more or less steeply depending on how far off the shortage was. The progressive rise in prices would have the dual effect of reducing the growth in demand and bringing on to the market additional supplies of energy from sources that were not previously economic. People often talk as though there was a specific (and ever increasing) quantity of energy that man must have, but this is not really the case. Figure 1 traces the course of primary fuel consumption in the U.K. since 1900. It can be seen that an average level of about four tons per head of coal equivalent persisted until the end of World War II with temporary increases of just over half a ton per head in both war periods and a reduction of similar magnitude during the slump of the 1930s. It is only since 1945 that the level has been rising strongly year by year. Growth of energy demand on the scale we have come to expect is not essential for our survivial or physical (or mental) well-being, but mainly for the continued pursuit of that rather elusive concept "a higher standard of living". If energy prices move up to a much higher level relative to prices generally, consumers have the choice of either making do with less energy and less goods and services that use up a lot of energy or doing without other commodities. And the more they use energy in spite of its rising price, the higher is the price likely to rise.

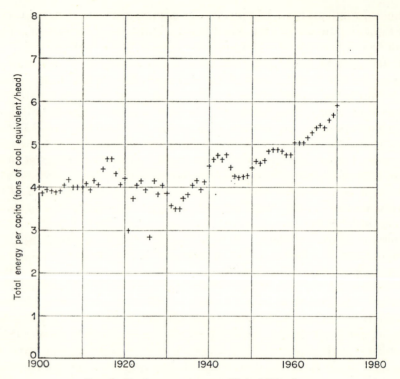

FIG. 1. Total energy *per caput*, United Kingdom.

Over the last twenty years there has been throughout the world an enormous growth in the use of oil and natural gas while the use of coal has fallen heavily in most countries of Western Europe and America. The use of coal in some other countries is still growing but throughout the world generally it is oil that is setting the pace.

On present prices, demand for oil and natural gas would certainly continue to grow fast while in most of the industrialized countries coal would continue to decline. Generally, oil and natural gas have advantages in convenience in use over coal and they are also cheaper to transport. In parts of the world where coal is obtainable cheaply, it is still holding its own but elsewhere it is very hard pressed to compete against oil and natural gas. Nobody can say with any certainty what is the total quantity of any of the fossil fuels in the ground; further discoveries are being made all the time and further information becomes available about deposits already known to exist. But there is now a very general belief that oil and natural gas reserves will not last very long if demand continues to grow as it has been doing. Until three or four years ago most experts believed (or acted as though they believed) that oil supplies would last for as far ahead as it was necessary to worry about, and prices were low relative to the potential value of the product: how high that value is, is indicated by the taxes governments, at the consumer end, find it possible to impose. But now there has been a great swing of opinion. An increasing number of countries are adopting conservationist policies and most countries are tending to raise their demands higher and higher. Unless views swing back again oil prices seem almost certain to rise progressively in real terms. Just how high they will go and what the effect on demand is likely to be is still a matter for conjecture. We, in Britain, will not be insulated from world trends in oil prices even though there now seems likely to be such substantial quantities in the North Sea. The oil industry is international in structure and North Sea supplies will only meet a small fraction of the demand in Western Europe.

The outlook for natural gas has many similarities with that for oil, and its price is likely to move roughly in step. It is not expected to have a major impact on the world energy outlook.

If oil prices do rise fast it will improve the competitiveness of alternative sources of supply and of other fuels and increase the amounts supplied from these sources. Coal would probably be a substantial beneficiary. Use of coal has not been restricted because of lack of reserves but because generally its costs of production and distribution were higher than those of oil. But the differences in price in competing sectors are fairly small at present in Britain and if oil prices go up a lot faster than coal prices there will be a marked change in the relative competitive position. Coal costs are likely to rise, here and elsewhere; even the mechanized collieries of today use a lot of men, and manpower is becoming an increasingly expensive resource. But unless the cost of manpower rises very fast coal prices are unlikely to go up as fast as oil prices in the longer term because exhaustion of reserves seems much more distant for coal than for oil. In the U.K. context this seems likely to mean a slowing down and perhaps a levelling off in the decline for coal. New coal production capacity is, however, inclined to take a long time to create and to be expensive so oil prices would have to rise a long way above coal's for there to be a major increase in coal production: this is likely to be true for the world generally (and especially for Western Europe) as well as for Britain. Although rising oil prices would have a major effect on the future of coal it does not look as though coal can have a major effect in controlling the rise in energy prices in the long run.

This brings us to nuclear power. Great progress has been made in the twenty years since the first steps were taken in the harnessing of atomic energy for peaceful uses: but this progress has been a lot slower than has at times been expected. Nuclear power is regarded almost everywhere as the fuel of the future but it is with us only on a relatively small scale at the present. If supplies of the fossil fuels start to fall off in the next decade or two, nuclear power would not only have to face a colossal task in building up sufficiently to meet the whole increase in demand for electricity but new nuclear stations would have to replace conventional power stations long before the latter are time expired. This implies a tremendous capital and resource commitment. If the expansion was based on a new type of reactor system the financial risks would be enormous unless the programme could be spread over a long period of years to keep them down to an acceptable level. A large nuclear component also implies that many of the nuclear stations would not be able to be used continuously all the year round, for which they are at present designed, because the summer load is a lot lighter than the winter load. Hence, under these conditions much more expensive electricity seems highly probable unless there is a real technical break-through in nuclear engineering. Even so, nuclear power in the forms which already operate would set a limit to the extent to which electricity prices might rise unless the discovery and supply of sufficient uranium to match a programme of the size and time scale envisaged in the previous paragraph—on a world-wide basis—forced the price up greatly. There must be doubts as to whether and at what price uranium supplies on this scale could be obtained, particularly if the expansion was very rapid. Fast breeder reactors will extend the potential useful-ness of uranium from the isotope U235 to the more abundant isotope U238 but at the moment they need to be linked with the U235 thermal reactor in order to expand capacity at the maximum rate, so they are unlikely to change the situation fundamentally. In any case, nobody believes the fast breeder will have arrived on a significant scale even ten years hence and its contribution twenty years from now will probably be limited.

One factor likely to limit the extent to which oil prices might rise during the rest of this century is the existence of vast additional reserves of oil bearing material in sources which are not commercially exploit-able on any scale at present. Notable among these are the tar sands and shales of North America. Extraction of oil from these sources is an expensive and capital-consuming business but as oil prices rose it would become progressively more economic and eventually a high level of production could be reached. But it has been suggested that oil prices would have to reach about double their present level (in real terms) before exploitation of the sources became commercially attractive on a massive scale. We cannot see any other source of energy being developed sufficiently during the remainder of this century to make any significant difference to the general picture we have painted.

About 80 per cent of the energy we use is supplied from static sources for which, on the whole, substitution of primary fuels is possible. The other 20 per cent requires some sort of mobility of the energy output. This mobility is largely met today by the internal combustion engine. Not all forms of transportation are similarly affected. Some ships for instance are large enough to be able to utilise small versions of land-based power stations. The tracking of the railways makes electricity supply from fixed sources economically feasible if the density of traffic is high enough to overcome the high capital cost. For small units of transportation, however, the internal combustion engine is ideal and it is not easy to find an economic substitute. The value that the individual places on the convenience of having his own means of transportation is borne witness by the continued rise in the motor car population and the apparent market insensitivity to fuel price change. The substitute for the internal combustion engine being considered by the scientists is the battery and electric motor. This allows the flexibility in primary energy sources by using the secondary fuel electricity to charge the battery. Electric vehicles already exist and their development on a large scale by, say, the 1990's certainly cannot be ruled out, particularly in areas where air pollution by road vehicles is a serious problem. The higher the prices of transport fuels rise relative to the price of electricity the greater the encouragement to the electric car. And conversely the greater the the success in developing the electric car (and hence in getting the cost down) the less the pressure towards higher oil prices. With both Japan and the United States putting a lot of effort into the development of the electric car, this could be quite a major factor—though necessarily some time ahead.

Some of the flexibility in siting power sources near to centres of demand is lost with some of the substitute fuels. Hydropower is capable of substantial development in some countries but this is often held up to await the building of new plant to utilize the electricity at that particular location. The transmission of electricity by line is worthwhile locally but does not appear to be so attractive over long distances. Solar energy might be thought to be another source with virtually unlimited potential but no commercial process for its large scale use exists at the moment and it hardly seems a serious contender for this century. Tidal power could certainly be harnessed on a fairly

TABLE I
Energy consumption per caput by final users (heat supplied basis)

	UNITED KINGDOM		
	1950*	1960	1970
1. Agriculture	8·98	11·48	13·46
2. Iron and Steel	118·73	135·42	129·20
3. Other Industries	225·62	272·27	313·64
Total Industrial Sector	353·33	419·17	456·30
4. Transport			
Railways	81·29	54·57	11·49
Road	58·68	87·57	152·67
Water	9·47	10·88	9·06
Air	4·24	15·24	27·57
Total	153·68	168·26	200·79
5. Domestic	259·95	275·44	263·51
6. { Public Services { Miscellaneous	85·17	46·99 } 102·00 55·01 }	61·96 } 119·83 57·87 }
Total Service Sector	498·80	545·70	584·13
All classes of consumer	852·13	964·87	1040·43

* Estimated from published primary input figures.

big scale but it is expensive and is only likely to emerge as a real force if other energy costs, including those of nuclear power, go up a long way.

Thus, in sum it looks fairly certain that energy prices will move up in real terms in the longer term, at least until there is a breakthrough in nuclear engineering. No doubt there will be major fluctuations around the trend line as there have been in the past. Whether the upward movement is fast or slow probably depends most of all on the extent of new discoveries of oil, and where they are located—and on progress in the nuclear field. If energy prices do rise rapidly we can expect that total demand will rise a good deal less fast than has been the case in recent years, and less fast than expected in most of the forecasts made in recent years.

Price increases may not be the only factor leading to a much reduced rate of growth in energy consumption in the future. In the next section

TABLE II
*Change in energy consumption per caput by final users
(heat supplied basis)*

	UNITED KINGDOM	
	therms/head	
	1950–60	1960–70
1. Agriculture	2·50	1·98
2. Iron and Steel	16·69	−6·22
3. Other Industries	46·65	41·37
Total Industrial Sector	65·84	37·13
4. Transport	14·58	32·53
5. Domestic	15·49	−11·93
6. Public Service and Miscellaneous	16·83	17·83
Total Service Sector	46·90	38·43
All Classes of Consumer	112·74	75·56

we propose to analyse the observed pattern of energy demand in the U.K. over the last twenty years and look for any indications that demand for energy is levelling off or might do so in the future. The views are highly speculative and have not been developed to the point where they could be used with any confidence and should certainly not be taken as the views of the Department of Trade and Industry. Table I shows the developing pattern of energy consumption per head by final users in the U.K. over the last 20 years in six sectors of the economy. The consumption of the first three (industrial) sectors, representing 44 per cent of the energy consumption per head in 1970, has increased by 29 per cent in the 20-year period while the remaining three (service) sectors have only increased by 17 per cent. The average increase in consumption per head of 22 per cent is less than the corresponding figure from Fig. 1 (of 32 per cent) reflecting an increase in the consumption of energy of the energy industries themselves. This is due mainly to the switch in demand from the primary fuels to the secondary fuel electricity. The absolute change in therms per head for each sector is given in Table II for each of the ten-year periods 1950–60 and 1960–70. From Table II it appears that, generally, the overall rate of increase of consumption at the point of sale is slackening. Both the industrial and service sectors show a slackening but the effect is more marked in the industrial sector. Undue attention should not be paid to the individual component contributions to the aggregate figure for the industrial sector, since the individual figures reflect the changing market values of the U.K. product mix and we only wish to study here the U.K. behaviour as an example of a mature industrial economy so that the product mix does not matter. The same comment is not true for the service sector as most nations would expect to be the consumer of their own service product. The negative value for the domestic sector for 1960–70 can be ignored since increases in efficiency due to fuel substitution can explain the decline in heat supplied without a corresponding reduction in the useful heat obtained by the domestic consumer and since the substitution for coal is nearly complete we may expect to see the domestic energy consumption rise again in the near future. The transport sector is identified as the runaway element in the service sector, its contribution accounting for 43 per cent of the overall increase. Reference back to Table I shows that road and air transport are the heavy users. It might be deemed fair to take road and rail transport together as direct substitutes for domestic travel and freight. Looked at this way road/rail only adds 2 therms per head into the figure of 14·58 for the change in 1950–60 but 22 therms per head into the figure of 32·53 for the change in 1960–70. Some explanation for this meteoric rise in consumption can be found from a quick look at the traffic figures of the road and rail industries. Subjectively weighting passenger miles to freight ton miles in the ratio 1:14 (i.e. 1 ton mile = 14 passenger miles on a simple weight basis) shows that the traffic on the roads and railways in 1960 and 1970 was as follows:

	10^9 equivalent ton miles GB	
	1960	1970
Road	39·6	67·3
Rail	20·5	18·0
Total	60·1	85·3

Dividing by the energy input in therms corrected approximately to a primary input basis, we can obtain an estimate of the energy efficiency of transportation as follows:

	therms/equivalent ton mile	
	1960	1970
Road	0·117	0·126
Rail	0·148	0·051

It can be seen that the relative fuel efficiencies of road and rail transport are reversed between 1960 and 1970 so that the effect of the public preference for road transport has meant that the fuel saving brought about by the railways' switch from coal to oil and electricity has not been realized. The average cost of substitution of road transport for rail is therefore nearly 0·075 therms per equivalent ton mile or 1½ times its actual fuel resource cost. The marginal fuel resource cost of substitution can be expected to be even higher.

Looked at in a similar way the corresponding figures for air transport are:

(Freight, Passengers and Mail)

	1960	1970
Traffic 10^9 equivalent long ton miles	0·44	1·24
Therms/equivalent ton mile	1·82	1·24

The improvement of 30 per cent in efficiency of fuel utilization over the ten years by the air transport industry is impressive since there is no substantial element of fuel substitution present and the improvements must largely stem from the use of larger aircraft. However, in 1970, the fuel resource cost is still ten times that of road transport and twenty-four times that of rail transport. Environmental considerations may not permit nearly such a rapid rise in these fuels in the transportation

D

sector to continue. But before anyone assumes that this may be the simple answer to all the problems in the energy field, we should point out that the same thing was being said more than fifteen years ago since when there has been a quite unprecedented rise in their consumption; and please do not put too much weight on the other figures in Tables I and II. Because some fuels can be used more efficiently than others a change from one fuel to another may mean a change in energy consumption without the user getting any change in output. We also need to take into account energy losses during production of a fuel. Electricity can be used with greater efficiency by the consumer but there is a substantial loss of energy in its production. The total energy figures for 1950, 1960 and 1970 are as follows:

therms/head

	1950	1960	1970
Total primary fuel input	1,251	1,413	1,652
Total consumption by final users	852	965	1,040
Average efficiency of conversion at production stage	68%	68%	63%

This downward trend in average conversion efficiency is expected to continue as electricity increases its market share of total energy. It is usually only the convenience of electricity that causes it to be used under present conditions when another fuel could do the job. This is not always the case of course. The microphone through which we address an audience can be powered only by electricity: coal or oil by themselves will not do the trick. But you will note that this is a non-essential use of energy which happens to have become a habit—and perhaps a bad habit at that. We could just as well speak a bit louder to make ourselves heard by a whole room or perhaps use a megaphone. So an enforced reduction in the demand for energy may not be too calamitous!

Returning to the theme of this paper, we shall try to draw our conclusion that there are potentially available adequate sources of energy to sustain a standard of living higher than any level achieved by past ages of man. However, the rapid growth of industrialization in the technically advanced countries is beginning to show signs of straining the sources of hydrocarbon fuels. We note that the process of energy supply and demand is intrinsically self-balancing in the long run by means of the price mechanism in a market economy so that the question of the adequacy for man's needs turns on the ability to maintain existing standards of living or whether we shall see a rise or fall in the future. We conclude that unless alternatives to hydrocarbon fuels are developed the standard of living will ultimately fall. Nuclear power, initially through thermal reactors and ultimately through fast breeder reactors, will give us a breathing space of perhaps a century but the longer term prospects rely almost entirely on the harnessing of fusion energy from hydrogen. Priority of some sort will almost certainly have to be given to research in this field because the current methods of investment appraisal place such long term projects at a disadvantage, but the consequences of failing to get results in the field could prove a disaster for future generations. In the meantime, it is still necessary to press on with developing the technology of nuclear fission power as this is the main prospective source for a considerable time to come.

Resources, Renewable and Non-Renewable

JOHN DAVOLL

The Conservation Society, Walton-on-Thames, Surrey, England

It is a curious fact that only recently have we begun to face the possibility that the resources of the planet are not unlimited. Consider, for example, the confusion between income and capital in resources prevalent among economists and industrial planners. Reserves of fuel and metals are treated as effectively unlimited, and the idea that we should plan for their eventual exhaustion would make nonsense of a great deal of current economic thinking. Because many economists find this prospect distasteful, they react by alleging that, although reserves of some particular metal or source of energy may indeed be finite, the eventual rise in price enforced by scarcity will lead to the development of substitutes, hitherto uneconomic.

This point of view was clearly expressed by Barnett and Morse (1963):

> Few components of the earth's crust, including farm land, are so specific as to defy economic replacement, or so resistant to technological advance as to be incapable of eventually yielding extractive products at constant or declining costs.

Such professions of faith are seldom accompanied by any understanding of the physical and ecological consequences of resource exploitation. Even the diminishing number of scientists with a similar faith rely heavily on shortening their view of the future to the period in which solutions to resource problems still appear relatively plausible.

Of course, the future is in a strict sense unknowable, and any recommended programme of action is bound to be based on explicit or

91

implicit value judgments of the importance we should attach to the welfare of future generations, since this will determine the degree of risk we consider it acceptable to subject them to. Clearly, one who looks ahead only 30 years will have a very different attitude to the proper use of the earth from that of someone who looks 300, 3,000, or 3,000,000 years into the future, and it is perhaps worth mentioning that even the last period is still less than one-tenth of one per cent of the probable expectation of life of the earth as a habitable planet.

When examining the consequences of exploitation of resources, it is essential to try to make a full environmental accounting; to fragment the situation is tempting, because it makes it both conceptually simpler and apparently less serious. The global picture, however, is more instructive. We know that there has been life on earth continuously for at least 3,000 million years and that this life has slowly changed the earth whilst extending its range and variety and itself changing in response to climatic and geological contingencies. This long duration has depended on the cyclic nature of biological processes, in which after a series of transformations, powered ultimately by solar energy, materials are returned to their original chemical state. Technological processes, by contrast, are mainly one-way, transforming resources into, finally, waste products, which may then lead to environmental problems by acting as pollutants for the natural processes of the biosphere and also by affecting the solar radiation balance on which the earth's temperature depends.

It is important to stress that pollution, which has received most attention for its effects on man or on his economic plants and animals, is not by any means the only or even the principal danger. More serious is the destruction of ecosystems by mining and building operations, and especially by replacing them with the relatively unstable monocultures of agriculture and forestry. Agriculture itself has become a highly technological operation, and the production of food crops uses large amounts of fuel and industrial products.

All the pressures generated by technology on the biosphere and on reserves of fuels and minerals are increasing rapidly as a combined result of population growth and increased *per caput* demand. Already an enormous latent demand exists in the implicit assumption of Western material affluence as the goal of a world population which is now virtually certain to reach 7,000 million, or almost double its present numbers, soon after A.D. 2,000.

This is the background against which the use of various types of resources must be considered. The application of modern technology has blurred the distinction between renewable and non-renewable resources; on the one hand the linking of agriculture to fossil fuel consumption has introduced a non-renewable element into what was previously, under the best conditions, largely a cyclic process depending on solar energy, whilst on the other hand it may now be possible to recover resources from wastes, previously discarded as useless. It must be emphasized, however, that this latter process of recycling will normally require inputs of energy from fuel reserves, as well as being accompanied by various undesirable environmental side-effects. It differs profoundly from the natural recycling mechanisms of the biosphere, and cannot provide a permanent escape from problems of resource depletion.

Nevertheless, the distinction is still used, and the food produced by agriculture and animal husbandry is typically regarded as a renewable resource. However, even a partial listing of the one-way processes now involved shows how unwise it would be to assume that even the present level of production can continue indefinitely, let alone go on increasing. The list would include simplification and destabilization of ecosystems by the use of monocultures and biocides, leading to lowered utilization of solar energy (Woodwell, 1970); use of phosphate fertilizers from limited deposits; use of nitrogenous fertilizers manufactured by using fossil fuels; loss of genetic reserves; erosion of soil; salinization of soil during excessive irrigation; pollution of the oceans leading to lowered marine productivity; widespread loss of wildlife by destruction of habitat; development of antibiotic-resistant pathogens in factory farming; sacrifice of aesthetic quality in the countryside in the pursuit of economic efficiency; pollution of water supplies by farm wastes and fertilizer run-off; all the pollution and consumption of resources related to the practice of mechanised agriculture and the manufacture of the necessary machinery.

The really important concept as far as use of so-called renewable resources is concerned is not the maximum short-term yield, but the sustainable one—the one that can be maintained indefinitely without loss of productivity. The same concept applies to the use of wildlife, including fish, and also to water resources; to remove more underground water than is being replaced leads to destruction of stream systems, and, in coastal areas, to salination as sea-water moves in. It is worth noting that the above argument is totally anthropocentric, and attaches no value to possible intrinsic rights of non-human species, nor to any presumed obligation to leave substantial areas of the biosphere unmanaged for the enjoyment of future men or their successors. To admit these considerations would reduce the sustainable yield available for present human use, and therefore the sustainable yield calculated in this way represents a maximum long-term one, and is almost certainly less than an optimum long-term yield, in which broader considerations are brought into the reckoning.

Energy represents an interesting case, in that whilst one source of energy is, for human purposes, available for ever without diminution, we are at present drawing mainly on sources whose amount is limited. The first source is, of course, the sun, whose energy is likely to be available at approximately the present level for some thousands of millions of years, and in a form which does not pollute the earth in its generation. However, if solar energy were harnessed on a substantial scale to drive one-way technological processes, these would eventually set limits to its use. Although of great ultimate promise to sustain a long-lasting civilization at a modest level of technology, its extensive use during the critical period of the next fifty years seems unlikely because of technical problems. Indirect use of solar energy as wind power, and particularly as hydro-electric power, is long established, but the latter leads to severe environmental problems of its own.

Of the carbonaceous fossil fuels, substantial reserves remain, particularly of coal. Reserves of oil and natural gas are much less, and shortages due to depletion are probable within twenty or thirty years. These will develop long before the wells run dry, as powerful industrial nations such as the United States, Japan and perhaps the European Community endeavour to secure the use of as much of the remaining productive capacity as possible. The United States in particular will become a massive importer of crude oil before 1980.

The environmental effects of exploiting the carbonaceous fossil fuels are of concern, both because of their magnitude and their multiple nature. Thus, the liberation of carbon dioxide alters the permeability of the atmosphere to incident, reflected and re-emitted heat radiation, and may produce significant changes in global temperature. Accurate prediction of these is not feasible, since natural variations in temperature and the ieffects of other technological and agricultural processes, some probably as yet unrecognized, would obscure what might be a long-term trend. Such a change would not be quickly, or even at all, reversible.

In addtion, other environmental effects of burning fossil fuels cover an impressive range, including air pollution by sulphur dioxide, dust, carbon monoxide, water vapour from cooling towers, nitrogen oxides, ozone and other constituents of photochemical smog, hydrocarbons and toxic metals present in fuels; water pollution by oil spillage, tipping of colliery wastes, rejected heat from power stations and industrial effluents and wastes in so far as they are related to the production and use of fossil fuels; land pollution by mining wastes and effluents; destruction of habitat and landscape by mining, oil terminals and pipe lines for oil and gas, tipping of wastes and power station construction.

Nuclear fission is capable of meeting substantial global energy demands for several millennia, provided breeder reactors are developed and low-grade uranium ores utilized; even granite may contain 60g/ton of uranium, so that each ton of granite can, in theory at least, provide as much energy as 160 tons of coal. Correctly operated, fission reactors do not release sufficient radioactive material to the environment to constitute a severe global threat, although some increase in human ill-health might result. The real problem lies in the immense quantities of long-lived radioactive wastes produced in the spent fuel elements, and poses in an acute form the question of our responsibility to the future. The conventional projection of world energy consumption for A.D. 2000 is 25,000—30,000 million tons of coal equivalent (about four times the present figure), and if a substantial proportion of this is provided by fission reactors, the world will be a very dangerous place. It will contain many thousand huge reactors, all requiring the most careful management, and producing vast quantities of radioactive wastes, dangerous for millennia, which will need to be stored in some form. To trust our somewhat crazy species to manage this situation for long without disaster requires a confidence which many would regard as foolhardy.

Apart from this, the environmental effects of using the energy generated and disposing of waste heat will be limiting, and this argument applies even if the relatively clean fusion reactor is developed and the deuterium in the oceans provides a virtually unlimited fuel supply.

Finally, let us consider metals as a typically "non-renewable" resource. Although they do not physically disappear when mined, used and discarded, practical difficulties mean that recovery from waste is rarely over 40 per cent, and usually much less. Once the "lost" material has passed into the general environment, its recovery presents difficulties and environmental costs that are seldom realistically evaluated. In practice, serious shortages of lead, tin, zinc and copper are probable within thirty years and are likely to lead to dangerous international competition for remaining reserves. Use of lower-grade ores as the richer deposits are exhausted leads to more widespread environmental damage and often to higher costs.

It must also be remembered that very large quantities of metals are already installed in existing structures in the industrialized countries. Merely to produce stocks at this *per caput* level for the world population of A.D. 2000 would exhaust probable reserves of some metals many times over and for others would require over one hundred years' production at current rates. Even highly-efficient recycling cannot solve this problem, since capital stocks are involved.

It is clear even from this brief survey that the existing pattern of resource usage is not sustainable, since it depends on one-way processes within a finite environment. Attempts to find substitutes as a particular resource is exhausted merely shift the load to other areas of the biosphere, and on a time scale too short for the environmental side-effects of the change to be adequately evaluated. The severity of these problems is exacerbated when the process of expansion has been built into the reward structure of the economic system, and as stated by Istock (1969):

> Thus there arises a contradiction between the practice of economics in industrial states and the requirements for stable ecosystems. The two are probably at odds at every point of contact, with human population increase a concomitant of almost every difficulty. So general is the conflict between human economics and the ecology of this planet, and so pervasive, powerful, and unswerving the dynamic of the industrial state that it is impossible to imagine a suitable industrial ecology under prevailing economic theory.

Because of environmental limits, therefore, a transition will occur from expansion to some other mode, which may be either a relatively steady state at one of many possible levels, or a series of oscillations; there are now sufficient warning signs to indicate that this transition will begin within the next few decades. The important question is whether it can be achieved in a controlled manner to a humanly satisfactory sustainable state, or in an uncontrolled manner under the brute pressure of events, with a probably severe reduction in the capacity of the biosphere to support life. To achieve the former will necessitate deliberate planning towards an envisaged goal; it will not occur by the automatic operation of the price mechanism, for the following reason. The present controls on economic behaviour generally operate on a basis of short-term evaluation, with a high rate of discounting the future, and are reinforced by equally short-term feed-backs in the political mechanism. Consequently, in a progressively deteriorating environmental situation it will seem preferable at each point in time to accept a little more damage than to face the problems of radical social and economic change. This temptation is particularly insidious in that the environmental cost exacted for each additional step along the road will usually take the form of a growing but indeterminate hazard or loss imposed on future generations—an ever-growing burden of radioactive waste, an increase of carbon dioxide in the atmosphere or of pollutants in the oceans—of a nature which extreme optimism will be able to dismiss as eventually remediable by hitherto unforeseen technology. This will remain true until the marginal effects of additional damage rise steeply shortly before collapse, by which time few options will remain and subsequent events will be largely out of control.

It is not difficult to envisage proposals for a physically possible scheme of sane long-term resource management; for example, the following were set out in the memorandum from the Conservation Society to the Working Party on Resources set up by the Secretary of State for the Environment prior to the U.N. Conference on the Human Environment in 1972. (1) Use of renewable resources at sustainable optimum, rather than maximum, levels. (2) Planned use of non-renewable resources so as to avoid sudden discontinuities on exhaustion. (3) Distribution of resources so as to avoid gross inequalities. (4) Refusal to foreclose the options of future generations. (5) A system for resolving conflicts between exploitation of resources and environmental values that takes all the relevant factors into account.

The application of these principles of resource management would entail profound social and economic change, amounting to a transformation from an economy maximising throughput of materials and use of energy to one based on maintenance of stock with minimum use of new material and use of energy. Nevertheless, the skilful use of technology to obtain the desired results with the utmost material economy, combined with a change in our present unbalanced emphasis on material possessions and display as the only valid aim in life, could make the process tolerable and the final state preferable in many ways to the existing one.

Unfortunately, there are such severe institutional, political and psychological impediments to change that an optimal solution is, in practical terms, not obtainable. In order to make the best of the present situation and facilitate a constructive response to our problems, however, the essential first step is to discard the facile and short-sighted optimism that tells us that the laws of economics will be all we need to manage the resources of the planet properly. Man's relationship to the environment is now approaching a critical phase, and to meet its challenges successfully will require a degree of foresightedness and tolerance that has been rare indeed in past human behaviour.

References

Barnett, H. J. and Morse, C. (1963). *Scarcity and Growth.* (p. 10). Baltimore: Johns Hopkins Press.

Istock, C. (1969). A corollary to the dismal theorem. *BioScience,* **19**, 1079.

Woodwell, G. M. (1970). The energy cycle of the biosphere. *Scient. Am.* September, 64.

Population Crises in the Past

T. H. HOLLINGSWORTH

Department of Social and Economic Research, University of Glasgow, Scotland

Population is increasing today in almost every country of the world, and even most *parts* of countries have an excess of births over deaths. All areas with reliable statistics show the same general rise in population for a long time past, and it is easy to assume that an increasing population is in some way a law of nature to which there can be few exceptions. Reliable statistics usually begin in a country, however, at about the time that its pattern of population change altered from one of fluctuation to one of steady increase. Modern population changes are very stable and orderly compared with the changes of the past, which were often much more striking than anything we find now. Although population projections are regarded as rather poor for predictive purposes, it is much easier to guess the population of Great Britain twenty years hence in the twentieth century than it would have been in 1347, for instance, when any extrapolation of current trends would have led to a figure of population in 1367 at least 50 per cent too high.

The great changes in population size in the past were mainly caused by occasional extreme mortality. Instances can be found in which fertility changes seem to be equally or more important, but they are rare. We can therefore concentrate upon the peaks of mortality, for which the word "crisis" is often used. Too few people, as well as too many, might be regarded as a crisis of population, and the sudden change from one to the other must accentuate the crisis. Such a change is almost invariably a reduction, since increase cannot be very rapid without massive immigration, but the rate of decrease caused by death has practically no limit. Nevertheless, crises of mortality were of several types, and they are worth a good deal of study since their intensity and frequency determined population change. There was no average level of mortality, only a combination of years of moderate and of very high mortality.

The most frequent type of population crisis was presumably the crisis of subsistence, at least if we go back far enough; there may have been an intermediate stage later, when such crises were rare but other types still persisted. The food supply ran short, and a large part of the population died before plenty was restored. The term "famine" is normally applied only to large-scale crises of subsistence, affecting one or more countries, or at least a large province (as, for instance, Bengal), but poor harvests for two or three successive years, combined with lack of transport, could easily result in an acute food shortage for all the poorer people in a village. The conditions producing poor harvests would tend to be common to several neighbouring parishes, but often did not spread very far. The immediate cause of death was scarcely ever simple starvation, but some disease, such as typhus, that is much more lethal when it attacks a population without a good supply of food. Two villages could be equally strained by lack of food, but one might escape an epidemic and the other catch it. Nevertheless, the more general crises of subsistence are the easiest to discover and discuss, and they must have had the greatest effects.

The main features of a typical crisis of subsistence can be outlined, although scarcely any actual crisis has them all. First, a population that had been increasing, or tending to increase, for a considerable time; it would usually be at the highest level it had ever reached on the eve of the crisis. The birth rate would be distinctly high, almost certainly over 40 per thousand, and possibly nearer 50. Second, a tendency for population growth to stop can sometimes be noticed, together with a moderate rise in food prices. This is merely an economic effect of an increased population upon a relatively limited possible food supply, and sometimes the crisis would break before conditions reached this point. Third, records of bad harvests, owing to rain, gales, frost, or diseases of the crops. One harvest in five might be noticeably "bad" for some such reason, but the stocks of the community would be able to withstand it if it occurred in isolation. About once in twenty-five years, two such harvests would follow in succession and this was often enough to trigger the crisis. Famines might therefore tend to be periodic (Everest, 1843). The years 1315 to 1317 were bad in most parts of Europe (Lucas, 1930), but since then European famines have been more local, although very numerous. The harvests of 1692 to 1694, for instance, were poor in many parts of France, with catastrophic results (Meuvret, 1946), and Finland suffered similarly in 1696–97 (Jutikkala, 1955).

The most immediate result was a very steep rise in food prices, but we find little evidence of emigration from the worst affected areas. In the winter and spring following the second bad harvest, when food stocks were at their lowest and the weather often bad, the mortality rate could easily rise to more than five times its usual level for several months. In parts of England, "to starve to death" means "to die of cold", and death from hunger and death from exposure cannot have been clearly distinguishable in many a crisis.

Conceptions (Goubert, 1954) and marriages (Goubert, 1960) usually fell during the height of the crisis, and a general depression can be inferred in every aspect of life. The average size of the household also fell during the crisis, for few households were extinguished completely although many lost one or more members (Kondov, 1965). Towards the end of the most acute period, however, marriages might begin to rise again. Mortality would fall sharply following the ending of the crisis, and this would be accompanied by a boom in marriages and a lesser boom in conceptions and eventual births. Many of these new marriages were of widows with widowers, each suddenly bereaved during the crisis. After about three years, the effect of the crisis on the population structure would scarcely be noticeable any longer, but the total population size would remain low. Food prices, of course, tumbled as the crisis ended, usually because of an eventual bumper harvest.

This crisis of subsistence is not, however, the only pattern of a crisis. Of the others, urban bubonic plague was very striking in the sixteenth and seventeenth centuries. Villages seem to have been rarely affected after about 1450, although the evidence is not clear, and West-Central France, at least, seems to have had many general epidemics of plague after 1450 (Favreau, 1967). There are certainly many shattering accounts of plague in the major cities of Europe. Naples, in 1656, is the most extreme example: 25,000 people are supposed to have died on one day, and 300,000, or two-thirds of the city's assumed previous population, within a few months; but this figure is not universally accepted, and 200,000 deaths would be more likely, out of a population of about 350,000. Although there were many highly mortal diseases, bubonic plague was the worst. It came in Northern parts of Europe about May and ended about November, reaching its height at harvest time. Migration out of a plague-stricken city was not uncommon, and the practice seems to have steadily increased as wealth grew and transport facilities improved. By 1805, this practice had reached the point where more than a third of the population of New York City fled when yellow fever broke out there, and only 1 in 200 died of those who stayed (Duffy, 1966). Many tradespeople in a city would not dare to leave their premises, however, whatever the risk of mortality, and many poor had, no doubt, nowhere to go. In all cities, we can assume that the great majority stayed to face the plague, especially before the Renaissance when transport was particularly bad.

In a rural crisis of subsistence, the poor were chiefly affected, but no age-group seems to have been especially vulnerable. The meagre food supply was presumably eked out amongst all the family, and neither old nor young, men nor women, bore the brunt of the famine. In an urban epidemic of bubonic plague, however, while the rich could leave and the poor were often obliged to stay, there could still be striking differences in the mortality of different age-groups and sexes (Hollingsworth and Hollingsworth, 1971). In general, children seem to have suffered the most from plague. Lacking any kind of acquired immunity from an earlier epidemic, children seem, in fact, to have been the chief victims of most of the violent epidemics of the past. As recently as 1918, the infant death rate in the Philippines rose to over 800 per thousand in Bulacan province (Philippine Islands, 1920), owing to the influenza epidemic that then spread over much of the world.

The effects of most urban epidemics were surprisingly slight. At Constantinople, it was the official policy to encourage repopulation after a plague had greatly reduced numbers, and elsewhere it rarely took more than three years for a city to recover. The balance was, of course, restored by an influx of healthy country folk, who might be eager to step into good jobs in the renewed city. Possible exceptions might occur when the toll of death was unusually heavy. The following list, beginning in 1348, is an attempt to tabulate all places of 50,000 or more that lost more than 25 per cent of their population in one year for any reason, as well as any smaller places that nevertheless lost 12,500 in one year. The list is, of course, incomplete, and some latitude in estimating both population and mortality has been necessary. The more doubtful cases are marked with queries, and some only have a bald chronicler's statement to support them. The principal source is Mols (1954–56), but many pieces of evidence have been weighed to produce this provisional list, grossly deficient as it certainly is for outside Europe:

1348:	Avignon, Bologna, Ferrara, Florence, Genoa (?), Marseilles (?), Messina, Naples, Padua, Rouen, Siena, Venice	1350:	Lübeck
		1360:	Avignon, Parma
		1361:	London (?)
		1381:	Lübeck
		1388:	Lübeck
1348–49:	Cairo, Gaza, London	1393:	Lübeck
1349:	Ypres	1405:	Padua

1405–06:	Lübeck	1633:	Breslau
1407:	London (?)	1635:	Leyden
1410:	Barcelona (?)	1642:	Kaifeng (?)
1417:	Florence (?)	1642–43:	Cairo (?)
1418:	Paris, Venice (?)	1650–51:	Dublin (?)
1427:	Danzig (?)	1656:	Genoa, Naples
1437:	Cairo (?)	1670–71:	Patna
1438–39:	Paris	1679:	Vienna
1449:	Strasbourg	1689–90:	Bombay (?)
1457–58:	Barcelona	1693:	Catania E
1459–60:	Cairo (?)	1703:	Tokyo E
1466:	Paris (?)	1706:	Abruzzo E
1468–69:	Tunis (?)	1709:	Copenhagen, Danzig,
1485:	Milan (?)		Stockholm (?)
1490:	Ypres	1710:	Krakow, Prague
1500:	London (?)	1716:	Algiers (?) E
1501:	Rome (?)	1720:	Marseilles
1507:	Cordova, Seville	1721:	Toulon
1527:	Rome (?)	1727:	Tabriz E
1527–28:	Florence	1735:	Cairo (?)
1531:	Lisbon (?) E	1743:	Messina
1541:	Constantinople (?)	1746:	Lima E
1549:	Königsberg	1754–55:	Cairo (?) two E
1556–57:	Brussels	1755:	Kashan E, Lisbon E
1563:	London	1759:	Baalbec E
1570:	Moscow (?)	1761–62:	Mexico City (?)
1576–77:	Mexico City	1769–70:	Bengal, including Calcutta
1577:	Genoa, Pavia (?), Venice	1771:	Moscow (?)
1578:	Louvain	1773:	Baghdad, Basra
1580:	Cairo, Marseilles, Paris	1794:	Cuzco E, Quito E
1585:	Breslau (?)	1817–18:	Algiers
1597:	Magdeburg (?)	1822:	Aleppo E
1602:	Danzig	1831:	Baghdad
1603:	Cairo (?)	1835:	Cairo
1618–19:	Cairo (?)	1877–78:	Shansi province (?)
1628–29:	Toulouse (?)	1899–1900:	Baroda state,
1630:	Bologna, Brescia, Cre-		Indore state (?)
	mona, Mantua, Milan,		Rajputana state (?)
	Padua, Parma, Piacenza,	1908:	Messina E
	Venice, Verona		

Several of these disasters were by earthquakes, and they are denoted by an "E". The 1769–70 Bengal, 1877–78 Shansi, and 1899–1900 Baroda, Indore, and Rajputana disasters were famines. The others were principally plague, many of them accompanied by a certain degree of famine. One may notice that the London plagues of 1603, 1625 and 1665 (the so-called "Great Plague") do not appear, since fewer than a quarter of the population of London died in them. There were certainly more deaths in Naples in 1656 and Vienna in 1679 than in London in 1665. The relative isolation and underpopulation of Britain evidently saved her from the worst disasters, and London was the only major city before about 1750. The calamity that struck northern Italy in 1630 also stands out very clearly in the record. The largest cities were not especially liable to extreme outbreaks of plague, since plague seems to have been partly a matter of chance and partly a matter of inefficient quarantine regulations. There were obvious waves of plague in 1348–50 (Carpentier, 1962), 1360–61, 1405–07, 1417–18, 1577–78, 1628–30, and 1709–10, in each of which three or more cities were affected in this extreme sense. Many others can be identified by epidemiologists, since even a 10 per cent death rate was highly calamitous and noticeable. There is, in fact, an abundance of material, but some of it, like Defoe's *Journal of the Plague Year*, is virtually fiction, for vividness of writing is unfortunately no guarantee of truth. From this kind of evidence, we can form an idea of the way in which people continued life, and even remained cheerful, at a time when 1 per cent were dying every three days or so.

In the cities, crises of subsistence did not occur in the rural sense, but famines were not unknown. Since city people normally drew their food supplies from a wide area, and necessarily had a regular system for transport of food to the city and for its storage there, a city famine rarely occurred. Only if a whole country or at least a very large part of a country, was affected, could a major city suffer famine but the effect would not then be merely for a few years, as in a city plague (Honjō, 1931). In general, famines on this scale have not happened since the middle ages.

A comprehensive study of famines in all parts of the world was made by Walford (1878–79), but it is now rather out of date. Germany (Curschmann, 1900), China (Mallory, 1926), Languedoc (Larenaudie, 1952), Ethiopia (Pankhurst, 1966), Russia (Pasuto, 1970), and Hawaii (Schmitt, 1970), have since received more detailed treatment. There are, moreover, numerous reports of famine, scarcity, or very high grain prices on specific occasions in the past, and numerous articles discuss them. (Bondois, 1924; Palanque, 1931; Gapp, 1935; Fergusson, 1939; Cook, 1946; Johnson, 1957; van Werweke, 1959; Hélin, 1959; Drake, 1968). We are told that the corpses could not be counted, that they could not be buried, that the living were inadvertently buried with the dead. The extremity of human suffering would seem to have been reached when cannibalism broke out. Only then can we be sure, retrospectively, that the famine was acute indeed. It is probable that cannibalism would be reported whenever it occurred on more than perhaps a few occasions, and thus we can distinguish the truly severe famines from what was mere hardship.

Vincent (1946) has studied the famines at Paris since A.D. 451. Those in which cannibalism was reported occurred in 850, 873, 940, 1007, 1027–29 and 1033. London seems to have been luckier: the only definite mention of cannibalism is in 1316, although the north of England resorted to cannibalism in 1069 and there was another English outbreak of it in 1239. There were famines on this scale in Cairo in 1070–72 and in 1201 (Lane-Poole, 1914; 'Abd-el-Latîf, 1202 and 1965). Cannibalism was reported in Ireland in 963–64, 1116, 1316, 1586, 1588–89, and 1601–03, and much of Central Russia, including Moscow, was similarly affected in 1602–03. Famines in India have often been acute, but cannibalism seems not to have become widespread except in those of 941, 1022, 1033, and 1790–91.

These illustrations show how frequent extreme famine was in a few relatively small parts of the world. Severe pressure on Paris was clearly a recurrent phenomenon, but the crusades seem to have helped drain away the population subsequently. London was, no doubt, saved from worse famines after 1316 by the great national decline in population that began with the Black Death in 1348. In Ireland, the wars of the seventeenth century, culminating in Cromwell's invasion, also led to a great reduction in population by 1659 (Cullen, 1972). The Irish famine of 1847–49 (Wilde, 1856; Cousens, 1962–64) was, in reality, on a lesser scale than the famines of 250 years before, and the absence of famine in Ireland between 1659 and 1816 except for 1740–41 (Drake, 1968), when the very cold winter afflicted many parts of Europe, shows how greatly Ireland had changed after Cromwell. In Russia, civil strife was the immediate cause of the famines of 1602–03. The government of the Romanovs, after 1613, prevented any repetition on a scale sufficient to lead to cannibalism.

Less severe dearths were much more frequent and caused considerable damage. They become ultimately indistinguishable from purely local crises of subsistence, but some were on a national scale. Britain seems to have had no such years after 1316, but in France the seventeenth century was an age of increasing famine (Meuvret, 1965) culminating in great disasters in 1693–94 and 1709–10 (Meuvret, 1946). Greece suffered from a substantial famine as recently as 1941–42 (Valaoras, 1946), precipitated by the War.

Population crises for which disease or famine were the sufficient causes are the classic cases, but we can also identify more general and less sudden declines in population. These usually were accompanied by a foreign conquest. The natural results, apart from deaths in battle, were new epidemics spread by troops, confiscation of property, ruinous taxation, and demoralization of the vanquished. The prime example is Mexico after the Spanish Conquest of 1521. The population dwindled, in a hundred years, to less than a tenth of its pre-conquest level, and completely changed the way of life of both peoples in two respects. First, they had to become accustomed to being fewer than in the past, with many useless buildings and redundant roads, and with much good land no longer cultivated. The possibility of discovering wealth accumulated in the past loomed larger than it might have done, and self-confidence waned. Second, they became used to a decreasing population, just as today we are used to an increasing one. Plans made on this opposite assumption usually mean that little need be done at all except maintenance of what already exists.

There are other examples. The rule of the Ottoman Turks had a depressing effect on the population of their empire, and both the Thirty Years' War and the Taiping Rebellion destroyed more than half the population of the wide areas over which they were fought. Ireland between 1641 and 1659, as already mentioned, is another example, and Indian towns in particular seem also to have declined (Habib, 1963) after the seventeenth century as British paramountcy replaced Mogul power. The Irish population decline since the 1847 famine, however, is a different phenomenon, and although its mechanism (late marriage and emigration) is well enough known, the underlying causes are still hardly understood (Leister, 1956; Cousens, 1961).

A population crisis was only felt to be so after it broke. On the eve of the crisis, despite obvious strains, the general mood of rulers and ruled alike was merely that another minor setback might be on the way. Some welcomed the crisis, moreover. The Black Death helped to create a scarcity of labour, and real wages eventually rose as marginal land went out of cultivation, creating many deserted villages, and rents fell.

Other common effects of drastic population decline were less to be expected by any section of society, however. During the second half of the fourteenth century in Europe, the universities lost most of their students and priests became scarce (Allyn, 1925). No doubt many young men saw the chance of getting their own farm who would formerly have taken orders. Religion declined, and morals (or so it was claimed) declined as well. The sixteenth century saw the recovery in both population and religion, and civil and religious strife prospered also.

Can we learn anything for tomorrow from this sketch of the crises of yesterday? Certainly, warnings of overpopulation went largely unheeded then as they do now; the shelves groan under the weight of

Reports on the Poor in Ireland, made ten or twenty years before 1847. Remedies were taken, but after the crisis had run its course. We always plan to fight the previous war brilliantly, not the next one, for we can analyse the past and correct it, but we cannot analyse the future.

Yet all need not be despair. We can study history to see the possibilities and to understand the kind of way in which events take their course. This can at least teach us to expect almost anything and we may have some idea of how to react to it.

References

'Abd-el-Latīf al-Baghdādī. (1202). (trans. by Kamal Hafuth Zand, J. A. Videan and I. F. Videan). 1965. *The Eastern Key*. London: Allen and Unwin.

Allyn, H. B. (1925). The Black Death: its social and economic results. *Ann. Med. Hist.*, **7**, 226.

Bondois, P. M. (1924). La misère sous Louis XIV—la disette de 1662. *Rev. d'hist. ec. soc.*, **12**, 53.

Carpentier, E. (1962). Autour de la peste noire: famines et épidémies dans l'histoire du XIVe siècle. *Annales (E.S.C.)*, **17**, 1062.

Cook, S. F. (1946). The incidence and significance of disease among the Aztecs and related tribes. *Hisp. Am. Hist. Rev.*, **26**, 320.

Cousens, S. H. (1961). Emigration and demographic change in Ireland, 1851–1861. *Econ. Hist. Rev.*, 2nd Series, **14**, 275.

Cousens, S. H. (1962–64). The regional variation in mortality during the great Irish famine. *Proc. R. Irish Acad.*, **63**, C, 127.

Cullen, L. M. (1972). *An Economic History of Ireland since 1660*. London: Batsford.

Curschmann, H. H. W. F. (1900). *Hungersnöte im Mittelalter. Ein Beitrag zur deutschen Wirtschaftsgeschichte des 8. bis 13. Jahrhunderts*. Leipzig: Leipziger Studien aus dem Gebiet der Geschichte. Bd. 6. Hft. 1.

Drake, K. M. (1968). The Irish demographic crisis of 1740–1. In *Historical Studies, VI*. Edited by T. W. Moody, London: Routledge and Kegan Paul.

Duffy, J. (1966). An account of the epidemic fevers that prevailed in the City of New York from 1791 to 1822. *New York hist. Soc. Quart.*, **50**, 333.

Everest, R. (1843). On the famines that have devastated India, and on the probability of their being periodical. *J. statist. Soc.*, **6**, 246.

Favreau, R. (1967). Epidémies à Poitiers et dans le Centre-Ouest à la fin du Moyen Age. *Bibl. Ec. des Chatres*, **125**, 349.

Fergusson, F. F. (1939). Famine and water supply in western Rajputana. *Geog. J.*, **93**, 39.

Gapp, K. S. (1935). The universal famine under Claudius. *Harvard Theol. Rev.*, **28**, 258.

Goubert, P. (1954). Une richesse historique en cours d'exploitation: les registres paroissiaux. *Annales (E.S.C.)*, **9**, 83.

Goubert, P. (1960). *Beauvais et le Beauvaisis de 1600 á 1730, Contribution à l'Histoire Sociale de la France du XVIIe siècle*. Paris: S.E.V.P.E.N.

Habib, I. (1963). *Agrarian System of Mughal India, 1556–1707*, Bombay: Asia Publishing House for the Department of History, Aligarh Muslim University.

Hélin, E. (1959). La disette et le recensement de 1740. *Annuaire hist. liégoise*, **6**, 443.

Hollingsworth, M. F. and Hollingsworth, T. H. (1971). Plague mortality rates by age and sex in the Parish of St. Botolph's without Bishopsgate, London, 1603, *Pop. Stud.*, **25**, 131.

Honjō, E. (1931). The population and its problems in the Tokugawa era, *Bull. Inst. int. Stat. (Tokyo)*, **25**, 2, 60.

Johnson, J. H. (1957). The population of Londonderry during the great Irish famine. *Ec. Hist. Rev.*, 2d Ser., **10**, 273.

Jutikkala, E. (1955). The great Finnish famine in 1696–97. *Scand. Econ. Hist. Rev.*, **3**, 48.

Kondov, N. K. (1965). Demographische Notizen über die Landbevölkerung aus dem Gebiet des unteren Strymon in der ersten Hälfte des XIV Jahrhunderts. *Etudes Balkaniques*, **2–3**, 261.

Lane-Poole, S. (1914). *A History of Egypt in the Middle Ages*, 2nd ed. Methuen: London.

Larenaudie, M.-J. (1952). Les famines en Languedoc aux XIVe et XVe siècles. *Ann. Midi*, **64**, 27.

Leister, I. (1956). Ursachen und Auswirkungen der Envölkerung von Eire zwischen 1841 und 1951. *Erdkunde*, **10**, 54.

Lucas, H. S. (1930). The great European famine of 1315, 1316, and 1317. *Speculum*, **5**, 343.

Mallory, W. H. (1926). *China: Land of Famine.* New York: American Geographical Society.

Meuvret, J. (1946). Les crises de subsistences et la démographie de la France d'ancien régime. *Population*, **1**, 643.

Meuvret, J. (1965). Demographic crises in France from the sixteenth to the eighteenth century. In *Population in History.* Edited by D. V. Glass and D. E. C. Eversley, London: Arnold.

Mols, R. (1954–56). *Introduction à la Démographie Historique des Villes d'Europe.* Louvain.

Palanque, J.-R. (1931). Famine à Rome à la fin du IVe siècle. *Rev. Et Anc.*, **33**, 346.

Pankhurst, R. (1966). The great Ethiopian famine of 1888–1892: a new assessment. *J. Hist. Med. All. Scis.*, **21**, 95, 271.

Pasuto, V. T. (1970). (adapted and translated by R. Delort). Les famines dans l'ancienne Rus' (Xe-XIVe siècles). *Annales (E.S.C.)*, **25**, 185.

Philippine Islands, Census Office (1920). *Census of the Philippine Islands. Taken under the Direction of the Philippine Legislature in the year 1918. Vol. II.* Manila.

Schmitt, R. C. (1970). Famine mortality in Hawaii. *J. Pac. Hist.*, **5**, 109.

Valaoras, V. G. (1946). Some effects of famine on the population of Greece. *Milb. Mem. Fund Quart.*, **24**, 215.

Vincent, F. (1946). *Histoire des Famines à Paris*, Paris: Librarie de Médicis.

Walford, C. (1878–79). The famines of the world: Past and present. *J. statist. Soc.*, **41–42**, 433, 79.

Werweke, H. van (1959). La famine de l'an 1316 en Flandre et dans les régions voisines. *Rev. Nord*, **41**, 5.

Wilde, W. (1856). *Census of Ireland for the Year 1851, Vol. V. Tables of Deaths*, Dublin.

Population Pressure on Resources: The Problem of Evaluation

JOHN I. CLARKE

Department of Geography, University of Durham, England

I have been asked to discuss the relationship between population growth and the availability of resources, or some aspect of this complex matter. This is no easy task, for the subject has attracted the attention of numerous scholars from Confucius and Aristotle until the present day, and therefore it is a well tilled field. On the other hand, the field is not static, for in industrialized societies in particular, the increasing dynamics of population and the increasing utilization and diversity of resources has complicated the relationship, which was already complicated enough. It is easy enough to say that population and resources are interdependent—that population depends upon a variety of resources, and the supply of resources depends upon what a society requires and is able to provide—but this simple statement conceals the many variables involved; not merely population numbers but also the characteristics of population structure, mobility and growth; not merely the quantity of natural resources but also their quality; and in addition the human resources, the skills and technologies to utilize the natural resources. And then there are the standards of living of peoples, their cultural attitudes and expectations, all of which influence man's perception and utilization of resources. These variables are associated with each other in interacting systems, which vary greatly in time and space, so that one can look at the relationship of population to resources at many scales from the world level to the individual locality over time and at particular moments in time. Thus it is worth while considering the problems of evaluating population pressure on resources, especially in view of the numerous generalizations made about it (Zelinsky *et al.*, 1970).

Territorial Identification

Unfortunately, the task is made difficult by the fact that it is often impossible to isolate or bound these interacting systems, and to relate the conclusions at one scale of analysis to those at another scale. What, for example, is a population? We are used to demographic measures without always considering the precise groups of people to whom they apply. We may define population as a number of people living in a territory, but what territory? So often the territorial boundaries bear little relation to population groupings, and people see themselves as living in groups quite different from those of administrators. Obviously the size, nature and delimitation of the territory greatly affects the numbers, density and structural and dynamic characteristics of the population, so much that the comparison of populations sometimes lacks validity. How meaningful, for instance, is comparison of the population data of China and Hong Kong? And then it may be argued that the territorial notion has less applicability as populations become more mobile. In these circumstances, geocoded data on a km square basis (as in the 1971 census of the United Kingdom) has perhaps more utility than data for administrative areas and enumeration districts.

The territorial notion also affects enumeration and evaluation of resources, though much depends on what we mean by resources, and of course definitions vary. Geographers tend to regard resources as substances or properties which satisfy human needs, and whether they satisfy human needs or not depends largely on the numbers and characteristics of the population in the area concerned. Although one cannot make any clear-cut generalizations about the effects of population growth upon economic development (Easterlin, 1967), in many cases increasing numbers have stimulated development, such as the intensification in some agricultural systems in tropical Africa (Boserup, 1965; Gleave and White, 1968). Resources also tend to grow with the aims, talents and efforts of peoples, with their economic and cultural attainments, and with their capacity to exploit them. Consequently, actual and potential resources may differ enormously. Moreover, increased technology and trading mean that not only are local materials brought into use but the area of the resource base is expanded, so that the resources available to a population are rarely limited to the territory in which they are resident, and the resources within a territory may be and frequently are exploited by an external company or country. Consequently in any consideration of the population-resource ratio there is a real problem of territorial identification.

The Search for an Operational Index

The problem of territorial identification has impeded all attempts to obtain quantitative measures for the population resources ratio, although other factors are involved such as the dynamic nature of population-resource systems and the reciprocal nature of their inter-relationships. It is one thing to produce a model of these interrelationships and another to produce a comparative measure. Ackerman (1959) for example, has provided a formula for population needs:

$$PS = RQ\,(TAS_t) + E_s + T_r \pm F - W$$

in which:

P = number of people

S = standard of living

R = amount of resources

Q = factor for natural quality of resources

T = physical technology factor

A = administrative techniques factor

S_t = resource stability factor

E_s = scale economies elements (size of territory etc.)

T_r = resources added in trade

W = frugality element (wastage, or intensity of use)

F = institutional advantage and "friction" loss element consequent upon institutional characteristics of the society

but he was concerned only with identifying numerous interacting elements within a complex system, rather than developing a quantifiable operational index. Other elements might be added (e.g. health status of population) and some qualified, but the difficulty of quantifying some of these elements indicates why a satisfactory operational index has escaped us so far. Moreover, if one considers that there is no single index which satisfactorily describes and distinguishes demographic types or regions, or even component elements like fertility, mortality and age structures, it is not surprising that an accurate population-resource ratio should be so elusive. This is one reason why terms like overpopulation, underpopulation, optimum population and population pressure are used so frequently—subjective terms which are difficult to define and quantify even in terms of single criteria such as standard of living or full employment—and why such criteria, along with others like soil erosion, out-migration, hunger and shortening fallows, are used all too often as indicators of population pressure or population-resource ratios, when other factors may be instrumental. To take but one example, soil erosion is sometimes used as an indicator of high population pressure, but may equally be associated with low population pressure (e.g. Great Plains of the U.S.A. and New Zealand).

The common use of such terms and more emotive ones such as "population bomb", the influence of diverse political and religious attitudes upon population-resource problems, and the appearance of lobbies concerned with particular variables like environmental pollution and family planning—these have resulted in general views being based upon specific aspects or cases of the relationship between population and resources. They also demonstrate that the population-resource ratio can never be dissociated from human perception; the demands, designs and desires of population will always remain an important factor in population dynamics and in resource utilization.

The Concept of Population Density

In view of the complexity of the population-resource ratio, it is perhaps surprising that so much stress has been laid on the concept of density, a concept derived from physics, where mass is related to the volume. But whereas the density of a gas enables us to make a number of accurate statements about some of the other properties of a gas, this is not the case with population density, where population is merely related to a measure of space. In calculations of population density both numerator and denominator present problems. The numerator may be the total population or a sector of it, such as the urban or rural or active or agricultural population, but it does not take into consideration any other structural or dynamic characteristic of the population such as age, sex and educational composition or natural increase. In general, it is a crude quantitative measure of population. As for the denominator, there is the problem already mentioned of the territorial units for which data are available—their size and their relevance to population distribution. Until the recent advent of geocoded data, density calculations and interpretation were complicated by the fact that data were only available for administrative areas or census districts which have varied in both time and space and have often been of little geographical significance in terms of uniformity or coherence. It is not surprising, therefore, that there have been many attempts to refine the notion of space in order to give some idea of its quality. So a variety of other denominators have been used, apart from total area: inhabited area, habitable area, rural area, cultivated area (sometimes weighted according to land use types), cultivable area, crop area, urban area, built-up area, floor area, etc. (Clarke, 1972a). By using such denominators the concept of density is modified from a man/land ratio to a man/land use ratio, for application among either rural or urban populations, but this does not make it a satisfactory index of population pressure. For example, areas like Western Europe and the Carribbean may have similar physiological densities: i.e.

$$\left(\frac{\text{total \quad population}}{\text{cultivable area}}\right)$$

or agricultural densities: i.e.

$$\left(\frac{\text{agricultural \quad population}}{\text{cultivated area}}\right)$$

yet have entirely different conditions of land use and population pressure. Similarly, how valuable are comparisons of urban land use densities of say Singapore, Kinshasa and Birmingham when the climatic, housing, social and economic conditions are all so vastly different? Although such density indices have value under not too dissimilar conditions, their value is reduced where environments, economies, and social systems are widely contrasted.

Critical Densities

Man/land use densities have been utilized in the consideration of critical thresholds above which there is said to be a deterioration of living or environmental conditions. Allan (1965), for instance, devised for tropical African subsistence societies a critical density of population (CDP) which was based upon a conservationist approach to population pressure. He defined it as:

> the human carrying capacity of an area in relation to a given land use system, expressed in terms of population per square mile; it is the maximum population density which a system is capable of supporting permanently in that environment without danger to the land,

or the density "beyond which degeneration leading to ultimate collapse is bound to set in". Allan used three sets of information in calculating CDPs:

(a) the percentage of land cultivable by traditional methods;

(b) the land-use factor, which is the relationship between the duration of cultivation and the duration of fallow; and

(c) the cultivation factor, or acreage planted *per caput* per annum.

Although the method has had some success among peoples practising bush fallowing methods of cultivation, it is not readily extensible to peoples practising other types of activity, especially where the inter-relationships between population and the environment are neither simple nor static and where they may be affected by numerous factors such as land tenure systems, methods of cultivation, cash crops, the health, mobility and growth of population, non-agricultural revenues and changes in social systems—some of which are difficult to quantify. Human societies today are rarely utterly isolated and rarely entirely dependent upon agriculture, and therefore although it is sensible and reasonable to try to assess the carrying capacity under traditional systems of agriculture, it must be remembered that these are critical land use densities rather than critical total densities. The notion that population density in developing areas is entirely related to land use has long been found inadequate, as the localized introduction of the modern economy has widespread ramifications causing massive mobility, improved technology and considerable diversification of incomes. Moreover, the idea that there are definable thresholds of population density above which mankind or the environment collapses is a simplification which has meaning only in circumstances of relative stability. In most of the Third World conditions of stability are rare.

Of course, the concept of critical density has also been applied to urban populations, with similar problems of analysis. As usual there are special difficulties with the denominator. Urban population densities may be calculated with respect to diverse areas such as (a) the total urban area, (b) the built-up area which excludes agricultural, unbuilt or unusable land, (c) the net area of occupied dwelling lots and incidental service uses such as garages, parking areas and play-grounds, and (d) the gross area of occupied dwelling lots, which also includes streets and parks. Obviously the results vary considerably and are only useful on a limited comparative basis, especially within a country. Planners also use dehumanized critical measures like (a) floor area ratios, which are designed to limit the sum of the gross area of all floors in a building in relation to the lot upon which it is built, and (b) the number of rooms per gross area, a measure which attempts to prevent congestion being caused by the construction of too many small rooms. In this country we are also accustomed to census data on persons per room, sometimes known as room densities, which have been used as indices of overcrowding, but they can give no more than a crude indication of urban densities because they neglect the height of buildings, the size of rooms, the provision of sanitary facilities and the composition of households.

Economic Density

While these critical densities give a rough idea about desirable limits of population numbers in particular sets of circumstances, they tell us very little about the relationship of population to resources. In an effort to compare the general situation in a variety of countries, a number of macroscopic measures of so-called economic density have been proposed, relating the population size to diverse denominators such as the gross national product, a general index of consumption, a general index of economic activities weighted in different ways, or average *per caput* income (George, 1959). Another way is to relate the gross product of a space and the number of people living in it to the income of that space (George, 1969). Unfortunately, the calculations for such formulae cannot be accurate or adequate, especially in advanced countries where the geographic origins of income may be extremely dispersed, as in the case of the profits of a large industrial company or a transport firm, or even aspatial, as in the case of many financial transactions or of pensions. And to complicate matters still further, whereas there is some validity in relating incomes to residential locations, this is less satisfactory for expenditures which are increasingly disseminated. Consequently, it is very difficult to spatialize the various elements of income or expenditure at district, regional or national levels, and thus territorial units are largely illusory in this context. In these circumstances it is perhaps inevitable that measures of economic density have remained macroscopic and of limited value for comparative purposes.

One general problem with all density indices is that they are essentially static, whereas the relationship between population and resources is very dynamic; they give only an instantaneous view of a changing situation. One might also argue that in generalizing population distribution into uniform areas the density concept runs counter to the recent trend towards increasing unevenness of population distribution, a trend associated with only limited and localized expansion of the ecumene (or inhabited area), with the rapidity and frequency of urban growth and with the diminishing links between population and land. Comparable with the patchiness of population distribution is the unevenness of resources, whose distribution is not coincidental with that of population, as we see for example in the case of a small town in this country, whose resources may be world-wide.

Scale of Analysis

As a geographer, I should like in conclusion to return to the question of scale, because it plays such a vital role in all considerations of the relationships between population and resources—at least it *should* play a vital role, for there are severe scale-linkage problems. Areal scale is particularly important, because for reasons already mentioned population-resource relationships pose different problems at the world, continental, national, regional, provincial, tribal, village or household levels. Nowadays it is fashionable and perhaps easier to consider the world as a whole (e.g. Forrester, 1971; Meadows *et al.*, 1972), because one is dealing with a closed population and a single ecosystem. The global perspective is certainly necessary and valuable, but global totals and arithmetic maxima conceal immense diversity and maldistribution of both population and resources arising from a multitude of factors, environmental, political, economic and social, as well as continuous but varied rates of change in different parts of the world. Such complexity tends to vitiate the global solution which tends to minimise human diversity and division and is over-simplistic, being only really meaningful in terms of world government. In these circumstances it is not surprising that viewpoints and attitudes to the global population-resources ratio vary enormously from the nearly panic-stricken alarmists to the sublime optimists, and that value judgements concerning human welfare, the desirability of economic growth and environmental conservation have important influences upon such views. It is also not surprising that the views of "haves" and "have-nots" should be widely different; one is very conscious, for example, that many people in developing countries view anti-growth economists and population controllers as imperialists or neo-colonialists and will have nothing to do with their growth models.

As one reduces the scale of analysis to the continental, national and more local levels, populations and resources are no longer closed—indeed, they are ever more open. Mobility tends to play a greater role in the population dynamics of small areas than of large areas with the result that population structures are more aberrant from the norm (Clarke, 1972b), and in addition the resource base of a small area tends to be proportionally larger than that of a large area. Consequently, although it may be easier to quantify population and resources within arbitrary areal units at a small scale it is more difficult to relate them in bounded systems and to disaggregate the world model. The call for a detailed and accurate world survey of population pressure on resources, area by area, may never really be answered, and we are left with the conflicting subjective views that we have heard so often. Does Africa, for example, suffer from population pressure? Herskovits, Kamarck, Bohannon, Boserup and Ewing believe not, but Hance (1970), Steel and others believe that it does. Similar diversity of views exists concerning population pressure in Britain (Taylor, 1970) and many other parts of the world. Such views will only converge if we happen to achieve greater unity of values and purpose, and better methods of predicting future rates of change. At the moment, we are making little progress in either of these directions. But the purpose of my lecture has been to emphasize that the search for an operational index of the population-resource ratio is like trying to describe landscapes in quantitative terms; it reduces the complex reality to meaningless units.

References

Ackerman, E. A. (1959). Population and natural resources. In *The Study of Population*. Edited by P. M. Hauser and O. D. Duncan, Chicago: University of Chicago.

Allan, W. (1965). *The African Husbandman*. Edinburgh: Oliver and Boyd.

Boserup, E. (1965). *The Conditions of Agricultural Growth*. London: Faber.

Clarke, J. I. (1972a). *Population Geography*. 2nd. ed. London: Pergamon.

Clarke, J. I. (1972b). Population in movement. In *Essays in Human Geography*. Edited by M. D. Chisholm and H. B. Rodgers, London: Heinemann.

Easterlin, R. A. (1967). Effects of population growth on the economic development of developing countries. *Ann. Am. Acad. Pol. Soc. Sci.*, **369**, 98.

Forrester, J. W. (1971). *World Dynamics*. Cambridge, Mass: Wright-Allen.

George, P. (1959). *Questions de Géographie de la Population*. Paris: Presses Universitaires de France.

George, P. (1969). *Population et Peuplement*. Paris: Presses Universitaires de France.

Gleave, M. B. and White, H. P. (1968). Population density and agricultural systems in West Africa. In *Environment and Land Use in Africa*. Edited by M. F. Thomas and G. W. Whittington, London: Methuen.

Hance, W. A. (1970). *Population, Migration and Urbanization in Africa*. New York: Columbia University Press.

Meadows, D. H., Meadows, D. L., Randers, J. and Behrens, W. W. (1972). *The Limits to Growth*, London: Earth Island.

Taylor, L. R. (Ed) (1970). *The Optimum Population for Britain* (Institute of Biology Symposium No. 19). London: Academic Press.

Zelinsky, W., Kosinski, L. A. and Prothero, R. M. (Eds.). (1970). *Geography and Crowding World. A Symposium on Population Pressure upon Physical and Social Resources in the Developing Lands*. New York: Oxford University Press.

The Galton Lecture 1972:

Economic Policy and the Threat of Doom*

J. E. MEADE

Nuffield Senior Research Fellow at Christ's College, Cambridge, England

I am an economist with no training in the natural sciences. You must not, therefore, expect me to tell you to what extent the threat of doom is an immediate and real one. The answer to this fundamental question depends upon scientific and technological assessment of such matters as the ultimate effects of certain ecological and atmospheric disturbances, the technological prospects of substituting one material for another, and the prospects of a more direct harnessing of solar energy. There is much disagreement among highly qualified natural scientists on these questions. An economist will not grudge the natural scientists their little squabbles; but he would be foolish to try to judge between them.

That there should be considerable disagreement between the optimists and the pessimists among scientists and technologists is itself significant. The scientific and technological problems involved are very numerous; many of them are far-reaching and difficult of solution; and, above all, the interrelationships between them are exceedingly complex. What will happen to human society over the next half century depends upon a very complicated network of feedback relationships between demographic developments, industrial and economic developments, technological developments, biological and

* This paper is a verbatim account of The Galton Lecture.

ecological developments, and psychological, political, and sociological developments. In each of the many sub-divisions of each of these separate fields experts are confronted with difficult specific problems which they have yet to solve; but in addition to these specialized problems there remains the basic problem of how the developments in these various fields react upon each other. We need to see the system as a whole; and in our present intellectual atmosphere of expert specialization it is precisely in such generalization of interrelationships that we are weakest.

Methods of studying feedback relationships in dynamic economic systems as a whole and problems of decision-making in conditions of uncertainty are matters to which economists have devoted a great deal of thought in recent years; and this must be my excuse for venturing to address you on this present occasion.

Having said that, I will beat a hasty but partial retreat. In this lecture I am going to consider only the basic economic interrelationships in discussing what we should do to meet the threat of doom. But I think that will be sufficient to give an idea of the principles involved in considering interrelationships in a dynamic social system, and it will certainly be enough for one lecture for one hour.

What then are the economic factors in the threat of doom? I take the work of Professors Forrester (1971) and Meadows (1972) at the Massachusetts Institute of Technology as the text for my sermon. As the total world population grows and as economic development raises manufactured output per head of population, the total growth of economic activity will, they argue, press upon three different kinds of constraint: first, the limited land surface of the globe; second, the limited stocks of certain irreplaceable materials such as minerals and fossil fuels; and, third, the limited ability of the environment to absorb the polluting effects of economic activity.

These are indeed three basic economic limiting factors. To these three the economist would, I think, be inclined to add a fourth, namely the available supply of man-made capital assets—machines, buildings, and so on. Each of these limiting factors has its own distinctive features: and although these features are rather obvious, I hope you will excuse me if I underline them because they have important implications for the devising of economic policies.

The first group of limiting factors, typified by land, I will call "maintainable natural resources". Consider a farm of a given quantity and quality of land. There may be room on it only for one farmer and his family at a time, if a given standard of living is to be obtained from its cultivation. But when farmer A and his family have passed on, farmer B and his family can enjoy it. There may not be room for two at a time, but there is room for an unlimited number of families provided that they succeed each other in time.

The pressure at any one time of population upon the limited amount of land and its effect in reducing output per head because of the so-called law of diminishing returns is, of course, the limiting factor which has been so prominent in classical economic analysis since the days of Malthus and Ricardo. The fact that it is an old and familiar idea does not mean that it is a false or an unimportant idea. On the contrary, it is very relevant indeed in the modern world. In addition to this straightforward economic law of diminishing returns, there are other non-economic features of the pressure of population upon the limited amount of land space which may give rise to serious human problems—for example, the psychological ills which may result from too close crowding together. As this lecture will be confined to the more or less straightforward economic problems, the tendency as population grows for output per head to fall as the amount of land per head is reduced must stand proxy for all the evils resulting from a scarcity of maintainable natural resources.

The second group of limiting factors I will call "non-maintainable natural resources". Consider a stock of 1,000,000 tons of coal. Suppose that a family must consume 10 tons of coal a year to maintain a decent standard of living and suppose that a family lives for 50 years. Then the coal stock will provide for the decent living of 2,000 families, no more and no less. Nor does it matter (provided the stock is already mined and available) whether these families exist all at the same time so that a human society of 2,000 families lasts for only 50 years or whether these families all succeed each other so that a human society of one family lasts for 100,000 years. If 10 tons of coal a year are essential for a family and if the stock of coal has a finite limit, then clearly any decent population policy through its birth control arrangements must plan, sooner or later, for the painless extinction of the human race; and, on the face of it, in so far as the supply of non-maintainable natural resources is concerned, it does not matter whether we have a large population for a short time or a small population for a long time. In this respect "non-maintainable natural resources" are very different from "maintainable natural resources".

The distinction between maintainable and non-maintainable natural resources in the real world is not absolutely clear-cut. Land of a given quality may be maintainable if properly farmed; but it can also be mined if it is overworked or allowed to erode, so that its power to satisfy wants is, like that of a stock of coal, used up once and for all.

On the other hand, by recycling the use of certain minerals an otherwise "non-maintainable natural resource" may be capable of being used again and again provided that its users succeed each other in time.

Nor is the distinction between natural resources (whether maintainable or non-maintainable), on the one hand, and man-made capital resources such as machinery, buildings etc. a clear-cut one. Land can be improved by, for example, a man-made drainage system; it is then a mixture of a maintainable natural resource and a man-made capital asset. Coal at the bottom of a mine must be brought to the surface by human action; when it lies as an available stock in the surface coal yard, it is a mixture of a non-maintainable natural resource and a man-made capital asset.

The possible scarcity of man-made capital assets constitutes a possible limiting factor which an economist would, I think, wish to add to the Forrester–Meadows catalogue. It is clearly not such a rigid limiting factor as the fixed and immutable supplies of natural resources. But it could nevertheless in certain conditions be the decisive factor. Consider a population which has a very low standard of living and is nevertheless growing rapidly. Because its standard is low it may be unable to save more than a very small proportion of its income without reducing its standards below the barest subsistence level. This may mean that its stock of man-made capital instruments can grow at only a very low rate, since all its productive resources, such as they are, must be used to produce goods and services for immediate consumption rather than to produce goods to add to—or even to maintain—the existing stock of capital equipment. If the population is growing at a high rate, capital equipment per head will be falling. At some point the availability of dwellings, schools, hospitals, tools, machinery, factories, etc. per head of the population may become so low that output per head falls below the bare subsistence level. There is a human crisis due to a lack of man-made instruments; and this crisis which might occur even though there was no shortage of natural resources and no pollution of the environment could be just as devastating as a crisis due to those other restraining factors.

The final limiting factor on economic growth is the pollution of the environment. This subject has until recently been gravely neglected; but as so often happens in human affairs, it has, I am very glad to say, rather suddenly become the fashionable subject for academic study and for political discussion. Its study needs the co-operative work of economists, demographers, and other social scientists with biologists, chemists, ecologists, and other natural scientists. I am not qualified to discuss the technical aspects of various forms of environmental pollution. I can only consider some of the main implications for the general principles of economic policy of the existence of these problems.

In the Forrester–Meadows models of the world community this problem is treated in the following way. It is assumed that industrial production pours out a stream of pollutants of one kind or another, the flow of which into a reservoir of pollutants, as it were, varies in proportion to the level of world industrial activity; it is assumed that the natural ecological and meteorological systems drain away and eliminate a flow of pollutants out of this reservoir, this outflow depending upon the amount of pollution in the reservoir. Thus the winds disperse smog, the waterways cope with sewage, some wastes are degraded by bacterial action, and so on. Thus the degree of environmental pollution rises if the flow into the pollution reservoir from industrial and other economic activity exceeds the rate at which natural cleansing forces are evaporating the existing pool of pollution in the reservoir. But it is assumed that beyond a certain point the atmosphere becomes so polluted that the action of these natural cleansing forces is impeded. At this point the outflow of pollutants from the reservoir no longer increases as the stock of pollutants increases; on the contrary, as the flow of pollutants into the reservoir raises the level of pollution in the reservoir beyond this critical point the outflow is actually reduced; and there is then a crisis due to an explosive rise in environmental pollution which chokes economic and other human activity.

This may well be a good model of the existing relationships, though, as I have said, I have not the technical competence to express an opinion. But in any case without stretching the meaning of words too outrageously we may perhaps then talk of environmental pollution as causing shortages of certain environmental goods—for example, it causes a shortage of clean air, or a shortage of poison-free fish, and so on.

With these introductory remarks on the general nature of the four basic limitations to economic growth—namely, shortages of maintainable natural resources, of non-maintainable natural resources, of man-made capital assets, and of environmental goods—let me now present to you a much simplified model of the dynamic interrelationships between these factors. My model is in its essence of the kind constructed by Professors Forrester and Meadows; but I have modified their models in two respects. First, since my intention is no more than to give you a very general impression of the sort of way in which they are working, I have greatly simplified the model, in particular confining it to the economic relationships. Second, I have in certain respects altered the structure of their model in ways which make it rather more congenial to an economist.* I warn you, therefore, that when I come to criticise and to comment in detail on my model I am not necessarily commenting on the Forrester–Meadows models.

I start then in Figure 1 with a model of the production system. In my figures solid lines represent positive and broken lines negative relationships. Thus in Fig. 1 Output per head $\left(\frac{O}{N}\right)$ is assumed to be higher, (i) the higher is the amount of maintainable natural resources (or Land) per head $\left(\frac{L}{N}\right)$, (ii) the higher is the remaining stock of non-maintainable (or Exhaustible) natural resources per head $\left(\frac{E}{N}\right)$, (iii) the higher is the amount of man-made Kapital assets per head $\left(\frac{K}{N}\right)$, (iv) the more advanced is the state of Technological knowledge (T), and (v) the the lower is the level of Pollution in the pollution reservoir (P). If N is the Number of persons in the population and L is the amount of Land, then land per head $\left(\frac{L}{N}\right)$ is the greater (i) the greater is L and (ii) the smaller is N; and similarly for $\left(\frac{E}{N}\right)$ and $\left(\frac{K}{N}\right)$.

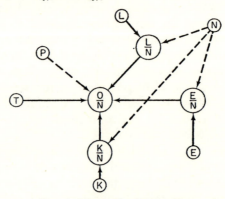

FIG. 1. The production system:

N = number of persons in the population;
L = amount of Land;
E = amount of Exhaustible resources;
K = amount of Kapital equipment;
T = state of Technical knowledge;
P = amount of environmental Pollution;
O = total Output of goods and services;
B = number of Births;
D = number of Deaths.

* Economists will, however, notice that the model which I present still has a number of glaring economic deficiencies. Quite apart from the need for greater disaggregation, which I discuss later, the production function which I use does not allow for increasing returns to scale; technical progress is an entirely exogenous factor, responding neither to learning by doing nor to investment in research and development; there is no proper savings function; the standard of living is measured by output per head and not by consumption per head; inequalities in the distribution of income are ignored; investment is assumed to be maintained at a level sufficient to give full employment; and so on.

In my Figure 2 I add the demographic relationships. ΔN represents the rate of increase in the total population and is the greater, (i) the greater is the total number of births (B) and (ii) the smaller is the total number of deaths (D). Three factors are assumed to affect the level of births and deaths. (i) Both total births (B) and total deaths (D) will be greater, the larger is the total population (N) subject to the forces of fertility and mortality. (ii) Births (B) will be reduced and deaths (D) increased by a rise in the level of environmental pollution (P); these are some of the links whereby a possible pollution crisis would show its

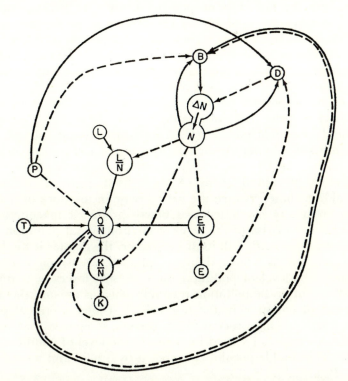

FIG. 2. The production system and the demographic relationships.

effect. (iii) A rise in the standard of living $\left(\frac{O}{N}\right)$ will reduce mortality (D). If standards are very low, a rise from the basic subsistence level is likely to raise fertility and births; but at higher levels of the standard of living, a further rise may cause a reduction in fertility; and accordingly in my Figure 2 $\left(\frac{O}{N}\right)$ is joined to (B) both by a solid and by a broken line. But if the standard of living should fall very low, then the consequential fall in births and rise in deaths will show the links whereby a crisis for human society is caused by a production crisis (a low $\left(\frac{O}{N}\right)$) due itself to a high level of pollution (P) or to low levels of maintainable natural resources per head $\left(\frac{L}{N}\right)$, of non-maintainable resources per head $\left(\frac{E}{N}\right)$, or of man-made capital assets per head $\left(\frac{K}{N}\right)$.

In Figure 3 I complete my simple model by showing the links whereby the total level of economic activity may react in turn upon the availability of non-maintainable natural resources, upon the stock of man-made capital assets, and upon the level of environmental pollution. Total output (O) is the higher (i) the higher is the total population (N) and (ii) the higher is output per head $\left(\frac{O}{N}\right)$. Non-maintainable natural resources are used up by the process of production and the rate of fall in the stock of such resources $(-\Delta E)$ will, therefore, be the higher, the higher is the level of total output (O). The stock of man-made capital assets will be increased in so far as output is not consumed, but is used to invest in new capital instruments; and in so far as people save a given proportion of their real income, the rate at which the capital stock will rise (ΔK) will be the higher, the higher is the level of output and so of real income (O) from which savings can be made. But machines like human beings decay and die and so, just as a large human population (N) means that there will be many deaths (D), so a large stock of capital goods (K) will itself, through the need to replace old machines, reduce the net increase in the stock of machines resulting from any given level of newly produced machines (ΔK). Finally the rate of rise of the level of environmental pollution in the pollution reservoir (ΔP) will itself be greater, the greater is the level of total output (O). As I have already explained, we assume that with a moderately low level of pollution the cleansing forces of nature will cause a flow out of the pollution reservoir which is greater, the greater the amount of pollution in the reservoir; but after a critical point is reached, the cleansing processes may become so choked that the flow out of the reservoir is reduced by a rise in the level of pollution in the reservoir. This double possibility is shown by a solid and a broken line joining (P) to (ΔP).

The interrelationships in Figure 3 are already complex enough in spite of the great simplification of the reality which it represents. Indeed the complexities are certainly too great for it to be possible to generalize about the future course of events merely by inspection of Figure 3. But in principle one should be able to tell the future course of all the variables in Figure 3 if one knew three things:

first, the starting point, namely the present size of the population (N), the present size of the stock of non-maintainable resources (E), the present size of the stock of man-made capital assets (K), the present state of technical knowledge (T), the present state of environmental pollution (P), and the present availability of maintainable natural resources (L);

second, the form and strength of each individual relationship shown by the arrowed lines of Figure 3—for example, the rate at which the stock of non-maintainable resources is depleted $(-\Delta E)$ by the level of world output (O);

and third, the future course of technical knowledge (T).

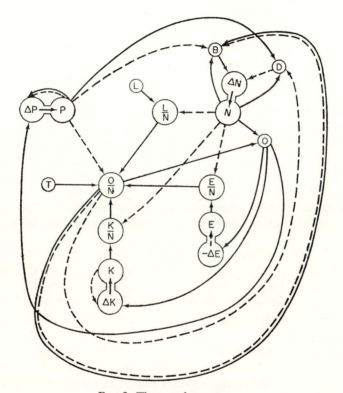

FIG. 3. The complete system.

For since one thing is assumed to lead to another in a determinate way, if we know where we start, how each individual variable affects each other individual variable, and how any outside or exogenous variables like T will behave, we should in principle be able to forecast the future movements of all the variables for an indefinite future time. We can instruct a computer to do the donkey work for us, and thus forecast the future course of world developments.

One can next examine the effect of various changes in policy by telling the computer to assume that at some particular date there is some particular change in some particular relationship—for example, that as a result of a birth control campaign there is from 1980 onwards a reduction of a given amount on the influence which the size of the population (i.e. the number of potential mothers) has upon the number of births. One can then observe the effect on the future course of all the variables of this change in policy, after taking into account all the dynamic interrelationships in the system. And this is, of course, just the sort of thing which Professors Forrester and Meadows do with their dynamic models.

It is not my intention to go through the various hair-raising scenarios for the future which they produce on various assumptions about future policies. These are important, but I must leave you to examine them for yourselves in *The Limits to Growth*. My immediate intention is only to comment on certain features of this method of studying the future.

There are some basic truths which Professors Forrester and Meadows emphasize through their work.

First, there must be an end sooner or later to exponential growth of population and output, and the limit to such growth may come upon us unexpectedly unless we are careful. The facts about the present world demographic situation which will be familiar to all of you are sufficient to illustrate the point. At present growth rates the world population doubles itself about every 30 years. If it were 3,500 million in 1970 it would be 7,000 million in 2000, 14,000 million in 2030, 28,000 million in 2060, and so on. Whatever the upper limit may be—and there obviously is *some* upper limit—we may hit it very suddenly. Indeed a mere 30 years before the final catastrophe we might be comforting ourselves with the thought that the world was after all only half full.

Second, the ultimate limit to growth may become effective either because of the exhaustion of non-maintainable natural resources, or because of pressure upon the limited supply of maintainable natural resources, or because of the choking effects of excessive environmental pollution.

It is good that these basic points should be forcibly emphasized. But it is not necessary to construct a complex dynamic model for their demonstration. Clearly scarcities of natural resources and the choking effects of an ever-increasing reservoir of pollution would set ultimate limits-to-growth. An elaborate and sophisticated dynamic model is needed not to tell us this, but to tell us how soon and how suddenly the limits will be reached, which limit will operate first, how quick and severe will be the effects of reaching a limit, how effective a given change in policy will be in mitigating these effects, and so on. It is to answer questions of this kind that there is point in trying to construct models of dynamic interrelationships of the Forrester–Meadows kind.

What will happen with any set of dynamic causal interrelationships depends in a very important way not only upon the extent to which one variable (e.g. the standard of living) affects other variables (e.g. fertility and mortality), but also upon the speed with which the various influences operate. Indeed, one very real cause for concern about the present situation is the recent changes in the relative reaction speeds in different sectors of human activity. Many changes, and in particular technological changes, have speeded up very greatly. Disease and mortality have been reduced at unprecedented rates. New synthetic chemical and other materials, as well as new technological processes, have been introduced at previously unimagined rates. As a result world population and world industrial production are growing at speeds hitherto quite unknown.

But while some variables are changing in this way at much greater speeds than before, other reactions are just as slow as ever and in some cases have become more sluggish than before. Many of the new man-made chemicals and materials are slower to decompose than earlier natural substances and thus their effects (which in any case are novel and only partially understood) may be persistent and reach into the distant future.

To take another example, demographic reactions cannot be speeded up. It still takes a baby fifteen years or so of dependency before it starts to support itself, twenty years or so before it breeds, sixty years or so before it becomes an elderly dependant, and perhaps seventy years before it dies. Indeed, with the raising of school-leaving ages and with medical advances which keep people alive and active to greater ages than before, these demographic time-lags have in some respects been lengthened rather than shortened by present-day technological and social changes. Their importance may be illustrated in the following way. The continuation of high levels of fertility combined with relatively recent rapid reductions in the rates of child mortality have meant that there is an exceptionally high proportion of young children in many populations which are now growing rapidly. In these conditions population growth would continue for many years even if the fertility of women of child-bearing age were to be reduced instantaneously and without any delay whatsoever to levels which would merely replace the parents. For many years, as the present exceptionally high number of young girls grew up to motherhood, the total number of births would go on rising in spite of this immediate dramatic decline in the fertility of each individual woman. Such a population might well grow for another two or three generations and attain a size one-third greater than it was when the dramatic fall in fertility occurred.*

To take one more example, political delays between the observation of a change and legislative and administrative reaction to it remain as long as ever; and indeed the increasing insistence on democratic consensus in government may have lengthened the time needed to make acceptable a political decision which has obvious present disadvantages but whose future advantages are not at all obvious to the inexpert man in the street.

It is not therefore a sufficient answer to the prophets of Doom to say that their cry of Wolf has been equally relevant since the beginning of time. It has, of course, always been true that exponential growth cannot continue indefinitely. But what is unique about the present situation is the unprecedentedly rapid rate of population growth and of technological innovation (which represent exceptionally rapid approaches to the finite limiting ceilings) in a situation in which the results of population growth and of technological change are at least as prolonged and as persistent as ever and in which the ultimate policy reactions to danger signals are at least as slow as ever. Such time relationships do, of course, increase the possibilities of catastrophic overshooting of safe limits; and dynamic feedback models are in principle the proper instruments for assessing the importance of the relationship between different time lags.

One must therefore sympathize with attempts to think in terms of a dynamic model of these interrelationships; but an economist can only contemplate with an amazed awe the assurance with which Professors Forrester and Meadows provide answers to our anxious questions.

The real world is a hideously complicated system and it is inevitable that any dynamic model should be highly simplified. To be useful it must, on the one hand, be sufficiently simplified to be manageable by modern techniques of analysis and computation; but, on the other hand, it must not omit any of the structural relationships which may have a fundamental effect on the outcome, and the form and quantitative importance of the relationships which are included must be reasonably accurately estimated. Furthermore, the future course of

---

*These demographic time-lags play no role in Professor Forrester's model, where no allowance is made for changes in the age-composition of the world population. But Professor Meadows has introduced them into his *Limits to Growth*. I am indebted to Professor D. V. Glass and the Population Investigation Committee for the population projections which are reproduced as an appendix to this lecture and on which I have based my statement in the text of this lecture.

certain outside, exogenous influences must be reasonably well predicted —a hazardous undertaking since it involves predicting the future effects of scientific and technological inventions without any precise foreknowledge of the inventions themselves; for if the inventions were already well understood, they would already have been made. These are very far-reaching requirements.

Economists—or rather that special breed called econometricians, in whose arts I am myself, alas, completely incompetent—have now much experience in coping with problems of this kind in searching for answers to much more limited questions. What is it which determines the demand for new motor cars? What is it which causes money wage rates to rise rapidly? What is it which governs businessmen's decisions to invest in new plant and machinery? And so on. But often, after the most detailed empirical enquiries, different hypotheses as to the structure of the causal relationships and as to the quantitative import-ance of any given factor in any assumed relationship provide conflicting results between which it is found difficult to choose even with the aid of the most refined statistical techniques. But the structure of the relation-ships and the numerical value of the parameters in a dynamic system can make a huge difference to the behaviour of the whole system; with one set of hypotheses the system may explode into a catastrophic breakdown and with another it may reach a stable equilibrium with or without moderate fluctuations on the way. But Professors Forrester and Meadows give results for an immensely complicated economic—social—demographic system of dynamic interrelationships for the whole world, having selected one assumed set of interrelationships and having used for each of those relationships estimates of the quantitative force of the various factors which in many cases are inevitably based on very limited empirical data.

For these reasons the conclusions drawn by Professors Forrester and Meadows are unquestionably surrounded with every kind of uncer-tainty. One must therefore, ask what is the moral for present policy decisions if the future results of present policies are still extremely uncertain.

This question can be put in a very sharp form by considering one of the conclusions reached by Professor Forrester (1971) in his *World Dynamics*. He very rightly emphasizes the fact that the ultimate effect of any given set of present policies depends upon dynamic interrelation-ships of the kind which I have expounded. Which influences work most quickly? To what extent are the evil effects of a given influence hidden at first and then operative with a cumulative, explosive effect? and so on. Professor Forrester concludes from his model that in order to prevent a worse ultimate disaster we should seriously consider the adoption of some very tough-line present policies. I quote from his book:

> Instead of automatically attempting to cope with population growth national and international efforts to relieve the pressures of excess growth must be re-examined. Many such humanitarian impulses seem to be making matters worse in the long run. Rising pressures are necessary to hasten the day when population is stabilised. Pressures can be increased by reducing food production, reducing health services, and reducing industrialisation. Such reductions seem to have only slight effect on the quality of life in the long run. The principal effect will be in squeezing down and stopping runaway growth.

In other words we might be well advised to forget about family planning, to discourage the green revolution in agriculture and the economic development of undeveloped countries and to let poverty and undernourishment play their role in restraining economic growth in the long-run interests of human welfare.

Professor Meadows dissociates himself from these startling recommendations for which Professor Forrester alone is responsible, but this paradoxical conclusion of Professor Forrester is not necessarily nonsensical. It could well be the correct prescription. But it depends upon a number of assumptions built into Professor Forrester's dynamic model. It assumes that while a successful birth control campaign may temporarily reduce population growth and thereby raise living standards, it is not capable of preventing that rise in living standards itself from causing a subsequent renewal of population explosion. It assumes that economic development will be of a given polluting character and that technology will not be capable of introducing sufficiently non-polluting methods with sufficient speed. It assumes that the effect of pollution is not a gradual effect, but stores up a cumulative reservoir of evil, as it were, until there is a sudden explosive catastrophe. If these assumptions are correct, then we ought perhaps to adopt tough-line present policies in order to avert ultimate, total Doom. One should perhaps be prepared deliberately to starve one person today to avert the starvation of ten people tomorrow.

But what if the outcome is uncertain? Should one starve one person today to avert a 99 per cent probability of the starvation of ten persons tomorrow? Perhaps, Yes; but should one do so to avert a 1 per cent probability of the starvation of ten persons tomorrow? Pretty certainly, No.

Much work has been done in recent years, notably by economists, on the pure theory of decision-making in conditions of uncertainty. In order to make a precise calculation as to whether a given unpleasant decision today is or is not worthwhile in view of its future potential benefits, one would in theory have to have answers to the following five sets of questions:

1. what are the different possible future outcomes of today's decision?
2. what probability should one assign to each of these possible outcomes?
3. what is the valuation—or, in economists' jargon, the utility—which future citizens will attach to each of these outcomes?
4. at what rate, if any, should we today discount the utilities of future generations?
5. what valuation or disutility to us, the present generation, is to be attributed to the unpleasant policy decision which we are contemplating?

One could then calculate whether or not the disutility to the present generation of today's unpleasant policy was greater or less than the discounted value of the weighted average of the utilities to be attached to each of the possible future outcomes, each outcome being weighted by the probability of its occurrence.

The models of Professors Forrester and Meadows are intrinsically incapable of such treatment. They are deterministic and not stochastic in form, although in fact they are steeped in uncertainty. I am not claiming that one could in any case make precise calculations of the kind which I have just outlined about the present uncertain threats of Doom; but I would claim that an appreciation of the principles of decision-making in conditions of uncertainty is helpful as a framework of ideas to inform one's hunches. My own hunch would be that the disutility of Doom to future generations would be so great that, even if we give it a low probability and even if we discount future utilities at a high rate (which I personally do not), we would be wise to be very prudent indeed in our present actions. But we should not, I think, be prepared to carry prudence to the extent of abandoning our efforts to control present births and our efforts to raise agricultural outputs and the production of other essential products in the impoverished underdeveloped countries, though we should be prepared to carry prudence to the extent of a considerable shift of emphasis in the rich developed countries away from the use of resources for rapid growth in their material outputs towards the devotion of resources to the control of pollution, to the aid of the poor, to the promotion of technologies suitable for both developed and underdeveloped economies which save irreplaceable resources and avoid pollution, and to measures for the limitation of fertility.

We may conclude that the failure to deal with uncertainties is a serious weakness of the Forrester–Meadows type of model. I turn now to a second serious weakness, namely its gross aggregation of many distinct variables. The model in my Figure 3 makes no distinction between events in different countries. It assumes only one output, making no distinction between different goods and services. It assumes only two uses of this single product, namely for personal consumption and for capital investment, allowing nothing for governmental uses for defence, space travel, supersonic aircraft, education, medicine, etc. It assumes only one form of pollution, making no distinctions between the pollution of air, water, or land or pollution by biodegradable wastes, by non-degradable wastes, by radio-active wastes, and so on.

This criticism is broadly true also of the models of Professors Forrester and Meadows, though they do both distinguish between agricultural and industrial production and Professor Meadows adds a third type, namely service industries. The introduction of this third distinction is also an important improvement. Services use up much less irreplaceable materials and cause much less pollution than does industrial production; and wealthy countries tend to spend a higher proportion of their incomes on services, thus providing a feature which mitigates somewhat the dangers of economic growth.

But all the models make no distinction between different countries, between different pollutants, or between different non-maintainable resources; and they make very little distinction between different products or different uses of products. This lack of disaggregation causes the models to exaggerate the threat of Doom in two important respects.

First, in so aggregated a model catastrophes are concentrated in their timing. Let me take the threat of a pollution crisis as an example. Let us accept the assumption that the evils of pollution often turn up unexpectedly with little forewarning when a reservoir of pollution rather suddenly reaches a critical level. In an aggregated model this must happen at the same time for every part of the world for every pollutant. *Ex hypothesi* remedial action is taken too late, and the result is, of course, catastrophic. But in fact atmospheric pollution in London rises unobserved to a crisis level in which smog kills a number of people; and belated action is taken to prevent that happening again; then the mercury danger reaches a critical level in a particular Japanese river; there is a local catastrophe; action is taken to deal with that; and so on. I have no desire to belittle these things or to deny that we should take these problems much more seriously than we have in the past. Nor, what is much more important, do I wish to deny that there may be some much more far-reaching, global dangers which are creeping up on us, such as atmospheric changes which will turn the world into an ice-box or into a fiery furnace. Natural scientists should be given every opportunity and encouragement to speed up their efforts to decide which, if any, of such evils is threatened by which of our present activities. All that I am arguing is that what in the real world might well take the form of a continuing series of local pollution disasters or of shortages of particular non-maintainable resources for which substitutes have not yet been found or of localized population control by a particular famine in a particular phase of development in a particular region are necessarily bound in an aggregated model to show up as a single collapse of the whole world system in a crisis of pollution, raw material exhaustion, or famine.

Second, an aggregated model cannot allow for substitutes between one thing and another, and some lines of economic activity use much more non-maintainable resources or produce much more pollution than do others. You may feel that I am making too much of a consideration of only secondary importance when I stress this lack of distinction in the models between different lines of production and different uses of products. Granted that there are some differences in the polluting effects and resource requirements of different lines of production and granted that economic growth may cause a shift in the relative importance of these different processes, yet, are not the shifts likely to cancel out to a large extent—some polluting processes gaining ground relatively and other polluting processes losing ground relatively? And, in any case, is not the net effect of relative shifts of economic structures of various industrial and other processes just as likely to be negative as it is to be positive on the balance sheets of pollution and resource requirements? In view of this, is it not perfectly legitimate to start with models which neglect such shifts?

An economist's immediate reaction is to point out that these models make no allowance for the operation of the price mechanism in causing one economic activity to be substituted for another. This point helps to explain why it is that economists are often less pessimistic than natural scientists in their attitude towards these problems. A large part of an economist's training revolves round the idea of a price mechanism in which that which is scarce goes up in price relatively to that which is plentiful with what in his jargon he calls "substitution effects" both on the supply side and on the demand side. Producers will turn to the production of that which is profitable because its price has gone up away from the production of that which is unprofitable because its price has fallen, while consumers or other users will turn from the consumption or use of that which has become expensive to the consumption or use of that which has fallen in price.

In so far as a mechanism of this kind is at work it means that the changes of economic structure that are brought about in the process of economic growth will not be neutral in their effects on demand for scarce resources. They will be heavily biased in favour of activities which avoid the use of scarce resources and rely on the use of more plentiful resources. How far this process will help to put off the evil day depends, of course, upon the possibilities of substitution throughout the economic system; and it is here that economists are apt to be on the optimistic side. When a raw material becomes scarce and its price goes up, it becomes profitable to work ores with a lower mineral content, to spend money on exploration of new sources, to use scrap and recycling processes more extensively, to substitute another raw material, to turn to the production of alternative final products which do not contain this particular material, and—above all—to direct Research and Development expenditure towards finding new ways of promoting these various methods of substitution. Indeed this process of substitution permeates the whole economic system. Family budgets are sensitive to relative prices; in India where labour is cheap and capital goods expensive clothes are washed by human beings but in the United States where the reverse is the case this is done by washing machines. Agriculture is intensive in the Netherlands where land is scarce and expensive and is extensive on the prairies of Canada where it is plentiful and cheap. Business enterprises succeed by finding a new process which, at current costs of the various inputs, is cheaper and therefore more profitable. Moreover—and this is of quite fundamental importance —commercial research and development is expressly geared to find new processes which economize in scarce and expensive inputs and rely on cheaper and more plentiful inputs; and technology, as we all know, can be a very powerful factor in modern society.

Some of you are probably losing your patience at this point. Is it any use fiddling with the price mechanism while the nuclear reactors burn? Has what I have just said got any relevance at all to the great problems of environmental pollution which constitute the major threat of Doom? It is in fact precisely here that we need a major revolution in economic policy to make the price mechanism work. Environmental pollution is a case of what economists call "external diseconomies". When you drive out onto the streets of London you pay neither for the damage done by the poisonous fumes from your exhaust nor for the cost of the extra delays to other travellers due to the extra congestion which you cause. When you take your seat to fly your supersonic aeroplane over my house, you are not charged for the noise you make. When you treat your farmland with artificial fertilizer, you do not pay for the damage done to my neighbouring fresh water supply. When in your upstream factory you pour your effluent into the river, you do not pay for the damage to my downstream trout fishing. When you draw water for that extra unnecessary bath, you are not charged extra on your rates—unless you live in Malvern where domestic water supplies are metered and so charged and where the inhabitants seem to live a happy and clean life with an exceptionally low consumption of water per head. When you put out that extra dustbin of waste for municipal disposal, you are not charged extra on your rates. If you were you might not merely insist on your suppliers reducing the unnecessary packaging of the products which come into your house, but you might also collect your glass bottles and offer to pay their users to come to collect them for recycled use.

I have, I fear, descended to rather homely and flippant examples. But the principle is the same for the most important and threatening examples of environmental pollution. We need politically to demand an extensive series of cost-benefit analyses of various economic activities and the imposition of taxes or levies of one kind or another at appropriate rates which correspond to the external diseconomies of these various activities. The price mechanism with its consequential process of substitution of what is cheap for what is costly could then play its part in the avoidance of environmental pollution just as it can in the economizing of scarce natural resources. Business enterprise will be induced to avoid polluting processes. Technologists will be induced to steer their research and development into the discovery of new non-polluting methods of production.

This is a vast subject fraught with difficulties with which I cannot possibly cope at all adequately in a short section of a single lecture. I can merely enumerate one or two of the main points.

First and foremost there are the problems of deciding what are the probable ultimate results of different forms of economic activity. These are matters primarily for the natural scientist and the technologist. Will the global effects on the atmosphere turn the world into an ice-box or a fiery furnace? And what are the probabilities of these outcomes?

Second, there is the problem of evaluating the social nuisance caused by a given degree of pollution of a given kind. To make use of the classical example of a factory belching smoke, how does one measure in £ s d—or rather pounds and newpence—the cost of a given output of smoke when some people in the neighbourhood don't mind it much and others cannot abide it? Quite apart from the question how one adds up these different individual preferences, how does one discover them in the first place?

Third, a great deal of the damage done through environmental pollution is future damage. The use of DDT may confer important immediate benefits without any immediate indirect disastrous consequences; but it may be storing up great trouble for the next generation or the next generation but one. Quite apart from the technical difficulty in determining what will be the actual effects on the future of this pollutant, how does one evaluate that damage? How does one weigh the interests of future generations against the interests of the present generation?

Fourth in most cases, if not in all, it is not a question of eliminating all pollution, but of keeping pollution down to its optimal level. I illustrate once more from the economist's favourite example, namely the smoking factory chimney. It may be prohibitively costly to eliminate all smoke, but not too costly to reduce significantly the output of smoke. To prohibit all smoke would leave the community without the smoke, but also perhaps without the product of the factory. To charge for the smoke the nuisance cost of the smoke might leave the community with some smoke nuisance, but also with the product of the factory. The latter situation might well be preferred. This is the basic reason for choosing, where possible, a policy of charging a levy or tax on the polluter which covers the social cost of the nuisance which he causes and then leaving him to decide how much pollution he will cause.

Fifth, in some cases—though these are much rarer than many administrators and technologists believe—it may be appropriate to act by a regulation rather than by a tax or charge on pollution. If the social damage is sufficiently grave, it may be wise to prohibit the activity entirely. I, for one, do not advocate discouraging murder by taxing it. But where it is possible to define and police a noxious activity for the purpose of regulating its amount, it is possible also to define and police it for the purpose of taxing it; and normally a tax on a noxious activity will be economically a much more efficient method of control than a direct regulation. Faced with a tax per unit of pollutant those who find it cheap to reduce the pollution will reduce it more than those who find it expensive to do so; and thus a given reduction in the total pollution can be obtained at a lower cost than if each polluter was forced by regulation to restrict his pollution by the same amount. Moreover, with a tax on pollution each polluter can employ the cheapest known method and, above all, will have every incentive to search for new and cheaper methods of pollution-abatement, whereas a direct regulation may well tie the polluter down to one particular method of abatement.

Sixth, in this use of fiscal incentives to avoid pollution, it is of great importance to tax that which is most noxious rather than to subsidize that which is less noxious. We all realize now that motor transport in large cities is causing intolerable congestion, noise, danger to life and limb, and atmospheric pollution. We all realize that private transport causes much more trouble per passenger-mile than does public transport. Both cause these troubles, but private transport causes more trouble than does public transport. The proper conclusion is to tax both forms of transport but to encourage public relatively to private transport by taxing private transport much more heavily than public transport. The wrong conclusion is to leave the taxation of private transport where it is, but to subsidise public transport in order to attract passengers from the private to the public sector.

Such a mistaken policy has an additional obvious disadvantage. We already need heavy tax revenue to finance desirable public expenditures, and I shall argue later that the new economic philosophy which we must evolve to meet the threat of Doom will make additional public expenditures necessary for such purposes as the redistribution of income in favour of the poorer sections of the community. The sensible thing for us to do now is to go round the whole economy taxing those activities which are noxious according to the degree of the social costs which they impose rather than starting to subsidise those competing activities which are somewhat less noxious. We can thereby help to kill two birds with one stone: we could discourage anti-social activities and at the same time raise revenue for the relief of poverty and for those other desirable public activities which we shall need to promote.

I have confined the points raised in this lecture to the use of taxes or other regulations to discourage economic activities which pollute the environment. In principle the same types of tax or regulation could be used to discourage economic processes which use up exhaustible materials; but I leave undiscussed in this lecture the question whether it is necessary in this case to supplement the influence of the market price mechanism which will in any case raise the cost of scarce materials. There is not time in one lecture to deal with every question.

To summarize, it is a mistake to rely on models of future world events which assume a constant flow of pollution or a constant absorption of exhaustible materials per unit of output produced. Economic systems in the past have shown great flexibility. If we were to make the production of pollutants and the use of exhaustible materials really costly to those concerned, we might see dramatic changes. Indeed, there have already been some marked improvements in the cleansing of local atmospheres and waterways in those cases where the first steps of governmental action have been taken. There is no *a priori* reason for denying that if appropriate governmental action is taken to impose the social costs on those who cause the damage, there could be dramatic changes also in the more important and more threatening cases of the threat of Doom through pollution or through the exhaustion of resources.

Such is the first fundamental reorientation which we need in our economic policies, namely to set the stage by fiscal measures or by governmental regulation which will give a commercial incentive to free enterprise to select a structure of economic activities which avoids environmental pollution and the excessive use of exhaustible resources. But given the structural pattern of the economy, pollution and the exhaustion of natural resources will also be affected by the absolute level of total economic activity; and this means that there must be restraint over both the rate of growth of population and, at least in the developed countries, over the rate of growth of consumption per head.

This last consideration points to the need for a second fundamental change of emphasis in economic policies in the rich developed countries. Much modern competitive business seeks new profitable openings for business by commercial advertising which aims at generating new wants or at making consumers desire to discard an old model of a product in order to acquire a new model of what is basically the same product. Thus the desire for higher levels of consumption of unnecessary gadgets and of new models to replace existing equipment is stimulated at the expense of taking out the blessings of increased productivity in the form of increased leisure. I have for long disliked the moral atmosphere of restless discontent which this creates. The discouragement of commercial advertisement by means of heavy tax on such advertisement and the return to broadcasting systems which are not basically the organs for the stimulation of new wants by advertisement could be helpful moves in the right direction. Moreover, some steps could be taken to give incentives to producers to produce more durable products rather than objects expressly designed to need rapid replacement. For example, if cars were taxed much more heavily in the first years than in the later years of their life, consumers would demand cars which were durable and did not need rapid replacement. In general, if a heavy tax is laid on the purchase of a piece of equipment and if this discouragement to purchase is offset by a reduction in the rate of interest at which the funds needed to finance the purchase can be borrowed, there will be an incentive to go for durability in the equipment. Less frequent replacement will mean a lower tax bill, and at the same time the value of the equipment's yield in the more distant future will be discounted at a relatively low rate.

The need to set some restraints on the levels of total production suggests yet a third basic change of emphasis in our economic policies. If we wish to improve the lot of the poorest sections of humanity, then either we must rely on rapid and far-reaching growth of output per head or we must rely on the redistribution of income from the rich to the poor. In recent years both for the relief of domestic poverty and for the closing of the hideous gap between standards of living of the rich, developed countries and of the poor, under-developed countries the emphasis has been on economic growth. The extension of social services for the relief of poverty at home has, we have been told by our politicians, been impeded by the slow rate of growth of total output, it being assumed that any relief of poverty must come out of increased total production so that all classes may gain simultaneously. The raising of standards in the under-developed countries must, we have all assumed, come basically out of the growth of total world output, so that standards in the developed countries can be raised simultaneously with those in the under-developed countries.

I have no intention of asserting that we should avoid further economic growth. Indeed a rise in output per head, hopefully of a less noxious form than in recent years, is an essential ingredient in the relief of world poverty. A glance at the arithmetic of national incomes is sufficient to show that it cannot possibly be achieved simply by a redistribution of income from rich to poor countries. But I am asserting that we would be wise to shift the emphasis significantly from a mere boosting of growth to a serious reliance on a more equal distribution of what we do produce, although we must face the fact that this inevitably multiplies possibilities of conflict of interest between different classes in society.

But as soon as we emphasize redistribution we are faced with a very difficult dilemma. Anyone who studies the financial arithmetic of poverty in this country—and I have recently undertaken a fairly intensive study of that subject—is driven inevitably to the conclusion that if anything effective and manageable is to be done more help must be given to the large than to the small family. However one may do this, whether by higher family allowances or by more indirect and disguised means, it necessarily involves subsidising the production of children. If we aim at shifting our philosophy from a mad scramble for ever higher levels of production and consumption of goods, however unnecessary they may be, to a more humane and compassionate society in which basic needs are assured, if necessary at the expense of inessential luxuries, we come up against the thought that our children, who by the way never asked to be born, are also human beings with basic needs and that the more there are of them in a family the greater the total needs of that family if every member is to be given a proper start in life.

The same basic dilemma shows itself in a somewhat different form when we consider the closing of the gap between the rich and the poor countries. It is the poor countries with the highest rates of population growth which will be in the greatest need of foreign aid and technical assistance in order to undertake those projects of capital development, (building new schools, new hospitals, new houses, new machines, new tools and so on), which are necessary simply in order to prevent a decline in the amount of capital equipment per head of the population. However disguised, does not this amount to the international subsidisation of those countries which are producing the most children?

Restraint on consumption per head is a means of restraining total demands on scarce resources which necessarily involves restraints on standards of living. On the contrary, restraint of population growth is a means of restraining total demands without any fall in standards of living. Population control may for this reason be put high on the order of priority for action to meet the threat of Doom, though it raises a basic ethical question which I cannot discuss today. At what level is it legitimate to maintain standards for the born by denying existence at current standards to those whose births are prevented? It would appear to me that, however one might answer this basic ethical question, the population explosion is now such that restraints on fertility should constitute our first priority as a means for restraining the growth of total demands on scarce resources of land, materials, and environment.

In many of the poorer underdeveloped countries the rate of population growth is exceptionally high; and their need for restraint is, therefore, exceptionally obvious. But there is need for restraint also of the less rapidly growing richer populations; and it should not be forgotten that one more American citizen because of his high level of consumption puts an immensely greater strain on world resources than does one more Indian peasant.

But while the control of population might make the most desirable contribution to the control of the total demand on resources, it presents in one way the most difficulty in its achievement. The price mechanism together with a proper, extensive system of pollution taxes by imposing appropriate pecuniary penalties can be used to restrain scarcities of material and environmental goods; these instruments provide powerful negative feedbacks in the total dynamic system. As the demands on material and environmental resources become excessive, so prices and charges rise to discourage demand and encourage supply. But with population, alas, it seems that we must introduce a vicious positive feedback. We wish to discourage large families; but on distributional grounds the larger the family the more we must subsidise it.

There is only one possible way out of this dilemma and that is to devise population policies which restrain population growth by means other than pecuniary penalties on the production of children. The first thing obviously is to enable everyone to avoid having more children than they want. Sterilization and abortion on demand, the development of family planning advice and services in all maternity hospitals, the complete incorporation of universal and free family planning into the National Health Service, the provision of extensive domiciliary family planning services, school education which inculcates that sexual intercourse should never take place without contraception unless a child is positively planned, governmental promotion of research into contraceptive methods—these are the first types of action to which we must devote resources to match any help which we give to large families. Whether or not we shall in the end be driven to consider more authoritarian methods is a question which need not be raised until we have fully explored the effects of a fully developed attempt at voluntary family planning.

I have, I fear, subjected you to a rapid and superficial survey of a large number of economic issues; and yet there is one vast section of my subject matter which I have hardly mentioned, namely the international implications of these problems. Before I sit down, I would like briefly to indicate one or two of the most important issues in this field.

First and foremost, there is the distinction between the rich and the poor nations. The less developed countries fear that the concern of the richer countries with the quality of the environment—a luxury which the rich can well afford—will for various reasons impede economic growth in the less developed countries—a necessity which the poor cannot do without. Past experience has shown that a recession of economic activity in the United States and other developed countries has hit the under-developed countries by reducing the demand for their exports and by reducing the amount of capital funds available in the rich countries for investment in the poorer countries. Might not a planned restraint on the growth of real income in the rich countries have similar effects in reducing their demand for imports, their foreign aid, and the capital funds available for the development of the poorer countries and, indeed, in leading in general to an attitude unfavourable to industrialization and growth in the poorer countries?

This fear must be exorcized. The stimulation of output per head in the poor countries is an absolute necessity for dealing with poverty in those countries. Such economic development is not incompatible with increased emphasis on population control, pollution control, and the recycling of materials. These things must not be confounded with policies to keep down the standards of living in the poorer countries.

A second set of major international problems arises from the fact that many of the problems which I have discussed cut across national frontiers. The supersonic aircraft of country A pollutes the atmosphere for country B. The whalers of country C reduce the catch for the whalers of country D. Country E may pollute a river, lake, or sea on which country F is also situated. Many of the controls which I have discussed will need international agreement and organization.

And finally there is the problem of international disarmament. It is not merely that nuclear, chemical, and biological weapons of war would, if used, represent the ultimate pollution of the environment. There is a much more mundane day-to-day consideration. The production of armaments itself constitutes an appreciable proportion of industrial output in the developed countries; and it is concentrated in sectors of the economy which make heavy demands on material and environmental resources. Moreover, there is a very heavy concentration in the richer countries of governmental research and development on weapons of war which, if turned to such topics as the control of the environment, might transform the outlook. Disarmament could make a major contribution to our problem.

The development of the will and the institutions for international action in these three fields is essential for the successful moulding of any set of effective economic policies to meet the threat of Doom.

References

Forrester, J. W. (1971). *World Dynamics*. Massachusetts: Wright-Allen Press Inc.
Meadows, D. L. (1972). *The Limits to Growth*. London: Earth Island.

Appendix

The Population Investigation Committee has in the following two tables made projections of the future population (1) in a country such as India in 1961 and (2) in a country such as England and Wales in 1961. Thus Table I shows what would happen to a population which started with the age structure of the Indian population in 1961 (i.e. with 41·2 per cent under 15 years of age) and with the Net Reproduction Rate of the Indian population in 1961 (i.e. with the N.R.R. = 1·865) on various assumptions about the speed with which the Net Reproduction Rate was reduced to unity from its 1961 level of 1·865. Table II carries out a similar exercise for a population which started with the age structure of the population of England and Wales in 1961 (i.e. 21·7 per cent of the population under 15 years of age) and with the Net Reproduction Rate of the population of England and Wales in 1961 (i.e. with the N.R.R. = 1·323).

TABLE I

India Type of Population (Age Structure of India, 1961: estimated N.R.R. India, 1961=1·858). Projections assuming varying speeds of decline of N.R.R. to 1·0. Single sex population, 1 million at point of initiation

N.R.R. 1·0 from:	Initial population 1 million	Subsequent population (millions) in					
		30 years	50 years	75 years	100 years	150 years	200 years
Immediately	1 million	1·275	1·331	1·329	1·331*	1·331	1·331
In 15 years	1 million	1·434	1·537	1·558	1·559*	1·559	1·559
In 30 years	1 million	1·532	1·771	1·843	1·843	1·844*	1·844
In 50 years	1 million	1·695	2·135	2·501	2·585	2·589*	2·589

* Point from which population is stationary.

TABLE II

England and Wales Type of Population (Age Structure of England & Wales, 1961 = 1·323). Projections assuming varying speeds of decline of N.R.R. to 1·0. Single sex population, 1 million at point of initiation

N.R.R. 1·0 from:	Initial population	Subsequent population (millions) in					
	1 million	30 years	50 years	75 years	100 years	150 years	200 years
Immediately	1 million	1·018	1·027	1·030*	1·030	1·030	1·030
In 15 years	1 million	1·066	1·093	1·111*	1·111	1·111	1·111
In 30 years	1 million	1·094	1·155	1·196	1·198*	1·198	1·198
In 50 years	1 million	1·128	1·228	1·356	1·392	1·396*	1·396

* Point from which population is stationary.

It should be remembered that the N.R.R. of 1·323 in 1961 is not realistic as a measure of marriage cohort or birth cohort replacement. The conventional N.R.R. yields too high a figure, being affected by age at marriage and proportions married: A more realistic rate would be lower and thus the population increases associated with slower rates of decline in fertility would be smaller than are indicated by the projections.

Service Provision and Local Needs

BLEDDYN DAVIES

Department of Social Administration, London School of Economics,
London, England

Measuring Service Needs

One cannot speak about service provision and local needs without asking oneself what one means by "needs": to assert that in the best of all worlds service provision should be highly correlated with service needs has no more substance than to assert that virtue should prevail.

An examination of the literature on social services yields a number of meanings of "need"—probably as many meanings as has "capital" though fewer than has "community". It is unnecessary to list these here: all that we are concerned with is the territorial dimension—the attempt to measure the needs of populations of areas. I want, however, to distinguish those intended to provide a basis for counting the number of persons judged (in some way) to require help, using social surveys, from those intended to provide the basis of an indicator of variations between populations of their relative need for help (judged in some way); and similarly to distinguish those intended to be specific to a service from those intended to be specific to a system of services which are substitutes for (or complements of) one another, or those which indicate a wide range of problems, attempts at whose solution might involve the use of one or more of a range of systems of services. In other words, this second dimension of classification distinguishes between concepts according to the specificity of judgments about what combination of services (and other action) is most appropriate.

Those whose aim has been to count the number of persons "in need" using information collected in social surveys have made an enormous contribution to our collective action by the discovery of the extent of handicap, of unmet needs in the community, of children from households with low incomes and of old people (Brown *et al.*, 1972; Bennett and Garrard, 1971; Harris, 1968; Harris *et al.*, 1971; Harris and

Head, 1971; Jefferys, 1971; Townsend and Wedderburn, 1965). Nevertheless, the conceptual and practical difficulties involved in using these techniques should not be underestimated.* First, there has been a tendency to define need as an attribute—to classify people as "in need" or "not in need"—rather than as a variable in which people are graded according to judgments about the intensity of their needs. This definition of needs as an attribute makes more crucial the value judgments made about where to draw the need margins: the boundaries between the states called "need" and "non-need". The results can sometimes be curious. One national survey concluded that the need for meals was four times greater than the supply (Harris, 1960). Four years later, a second national survey concluded that the need for the service was five times greater than the supply (Townsend and Wedderburn, 1965). In the interim, the supply of meals had trebled or quadrupled. Judgments about the need margins to accept must always be important, and have an element of arbitrariness; but it is important to use what devices are available to reduce the importance of the most arbitrary of them. Thus respondents' descriptions of their capacities and their statements about their own needs for services are frequently used as the basis of estimating indicators. However, as some of those who use these data as the basis of their estimates show, these are very likely to be influenced by a number of factors—factors connected with expectations, personality, and other things including factors connected with the dynamics of the interview situation.

These biasing factors are likely to distort a picture of geographical variations in the needs for services unless some way can be found of controlling their influence. This is particularly important since the work indicates that people have very primitive conceptions of the roles of services and have to be educated in their use; and their non-demand is influenced by a wide range of experiences and perceptions. Our perception of the dependence of demand on supply in the personal social services has been increasingly strengthened by the evidence accumulated in recent years. It implies that the mere estimation of numbers is insufficient: the effects of subtle changes must be understood. To take these relationships into account requires the use of a wider and more elaborate armoury of techniques—the more sophisticated and sensitive use of attitude testing and related devices for statistical analysis, and the greater and more explicit use of validated theory. The techniques for assessing why people do not demand services when they are eligible for them are still in their infancy. Only

* See note on p. 158.

when we have developed these shall we be able to tackle the separate task of estimating the number of persons who can be induced to demand by various forms of action.

Moreover, respondents' views about the extent of service provision that would just meet their needs is not evidence of the same nature as evidence about their need-generating characteristics. The need margins at which recipients feel that the supply would be adequate are tantamount to the estimate of the demand for a non-public and non-merit good at zero price; that is, to an estimate of demand at its satiety level for the good, if it were in the private market. Of course, most personal social services are not private goods provided in market situations. Most social welfare services are what (some) economists would call "merit" goods, since in the relatively few cases in which prices are charged, the service is almost invariably subsidised. (Musgrave, 1959; Head, 1966). The demand for these goods is a demand exercised by society as a whole. One should therefore ask a cross-section of the population what need margin they would wish to adopt for a service if one wishes to estimate the appropriate margin at society's satiety level. It is arguable that society cannot satisfy the demand for all commodities to the satiety level, and there is no reason why it should choose to do so for publicly provided goods only. Indeed, the public does not seem to rate social welfare service higher in its system of priorities than many other goods. For instance, a recent survey found that 67 per cent of a sample agreed with a proposition that too many people still lived in poverty, but only 24 per cent thought that spending on the poor should be among the first four things that most needed to be done in the 1970s (Barker and Harvey, 1969). If one wishes to discover the need margin which society thinks should really be provided, one should find out the lowest need margin the members of society would be prepared to pay for given its resource implications. Experiments have been tried which are of use in assessing the position of these margins (Hoinville, 1971). Inevitably, for most services—including, it would seem from the survey evidence quoted above, some social services—this would be a margin higher than the first margin.*

---

* In order to minimize its complexity, this discussion of the margins assumes that units of the service are indivisible, so that increased extensiveness cannot be offset by reduced intensiveness of provision. This is an assumption that certainly cannot be made in the long run for any service, and cannot be made in the short run for most. Making the assumption implies that any gap between the two margins would have the effect that, when steps are taken to give services to those eligible but not receiving them, the operational need margin will be adjusted in an upward direction. Therefore one cannot automatically assume, as some organisers of surveys into needs seem to do, that the operational margin would remain unchanged if the number of persons expected to demand the service had been equal to the number of persons who were supra-marginal at that margin but who had not been receiving it, in addition to the number who had actually been receiving it.

Thus the information collected in social surveys about the needs of recipients and potential recipients, although valuable as it stands, should be supplemented with other information, since it does not, by itself, throw light on the demand for what are merit or public goods. It merely provides information which may—indeed, I think, should—influence this demand. We all hope that this influence will be powerful. But the demand itself is one which has to be determined by the political system. Judgments ultimately have to be legitimated by the political process. Certainly those who are measuring need as agents of central or local government should seek to use judgments that have been thus legitimated. Increasingly, need measurement is done by such agents—research workers in social service departments of local authorities, research workers in independent research agencies working under contract to the central government.

At the present state of development, a proliferation of surveys into "needs" at the local level may be much less fruitful than alternative forms of research. One must not forget that the collection of survey data on a worthwhile scale is necessarily expensive. One must certainly avoid culs-de-sac if they have to be built to motorway standards. To make the best use of the data, surveys should be linked to models that estimate relationships between supply, demand and need-generating characteristics in systems of services, as shown by cheaper data potentially available from local authority and other files and other sources—in particular censuses of population. In this way, the gap between surveys in a few areas and the circumstances of other authorities can be bridged. For this bridge to be built, large surveys will have to collect information that can be linked to the other data that is potentially available; and should be conducted within a design intended to reflect the situation in areas chosen to represent permutations of condition relevant to variations in the principal relationships it is hoped to quantify.

The second type of indicator, based principally on collections of data in censuses and in local authority files, is intended to indicate the relative needs of areas and their populations. A judgment that seems usually to be implicit in this type of indicator is that characteristics of people and areas that have in the past been powerful correlates of the judgments about service allocations of those who actually make decisions as agents of the local authority are good evidence about democratically-legitimated need judgments in the future (Davies, 1968). They also depend on other forms of support. Such indicators are probably more valuable for the central government monitoring of local performance than for the specification of small areas of intensive social need within authorities themselves. A broad rather than detailed understanding is necessary for monitoring central-local relations, and so a small number of indicators of the theoretically most relevant factors will suffice. Indeed, too much information can be an embarrassment; a superabundance of data that cannot be effectively used offends against the cybernetician's law of requisite variety as much as the insufficiency of information. However, to select small areas for intensive help (under, for instance, The Urban Aid Programme) seems to me to be far more difficult. Craig and Driver (1972) have shown that it is feasible in one exercise to distinguish small areas where material environment is handicapping for the whole community. The Planning Department of Liverpool City Council have pioneered new ways of doing the same.

It is desirable to be able to use data which depend upon multivariate counts: examples are the number of long-term unemployed males aged 55 and over, the number of children in households receiving Family Income Supplements (or tax credits), and the number of elderly supplementary pension receivers living alone or with someone of the same age. A useful start in this respect would be to have some multivariate counts made available on the census summary sheets for enumeration districts: for example, the number of single or divorced aged persons enumerated as Social Class V living alone or with someone of a similar age in a household without the exclusive use of a hot water tap and an indoor water closet; the number of children of mothers born in India, Pakistan or Uganda from households living at more than $1\frac{1}{2}$ persons per room; the number of children in households living at more than $1\frac{1}{2}$ persons per room with only one adult who have lived at the address for less than two years; and the number of children in households living at more than $1\frac{1}{2}$ persons per room with only one adult who have lived within the administrative area for less than five years. A reliance on sampling—or rather sampling with constant sampling fractions—in censuses can make such indicators less reliable than they used to be. There is a good case for taking high or 100 per cent sampling fractions for districts within wards of special interest to local authorities. Some data available from other local authority departments and associated agencies are more readily available. The evidence of the Liverpool Social Malaise Study demonstrated the potential importance of police data on thefts, burglaries, malicious damage, assaults, motoring offences, offences of morality and other crimes, and court data on possession orders, debtors and electricity board warrants; the number of children deloused by the Public Health Department, the illegitimate birth rate, job instability, school absenteeism, free school meals, school clothing grants, the incidence of ESN

F

children, adult subnormality and children in care, and many other factors (Martin *et al.*, 1973). One of the crucial questions is the degree to which data on social security benefits can be made available for small areas. Some of the important data would require area coding at local offices. At a time when local officers are working much compulsory overtime, this must be planned for the intermediate term rather than the short term, even if, perhaps, postal codes were used to designate areas. Other data are analysed at Newcastle on a sample basis. A larger sample or a census analysis would be required to yield estimates of value for small areas. The receipt of some benefits are comparatively rare attributes in a population and their enumeration is unlikely to yield much for the identification of "needle-point" areas of social need. However, their enumeration will be of value for indicators for wider areas. After 1974, local authorities' own monitoring of the degree of territorial justice between areas with substantial populations within local authority jurisdiction will be almost as important as monitoring the degree of territorial justice as between administrative areas or the discovery of small areas of intense needs.

Possibly, the theoretical problems of diagnosing the small areas with the gravest social problems are less serious than those of choosing appropriate policies for collective action in the areas. Such areas are diverse, having different problems from one another. I therefore think that the theoretical basis for the classification of areas is more primitive than for indicators linked with well-established systems of services. Among the theoretical advances required are typologies that relate the characteristics of areas to new perceptions of the role of a broad range of services as substitutes and complements. The foundations for this theoretical advance have been laid by such diverse groups as planners, urban sociologists, economists of housing and others. But although directly relevant, the work so far done does not itself provide an adequate body of quantified theory that can be used in the field. There is therefore an urgent need for research to trace what happens to people in need in such areas, what services they have contact with, and how salient these services are to their needs and their perceptions of them.

Meanwhile I see the possibility of political conflicts arising when some areas are greatly favoured compared with others which are not very different but which in a binary classification of areas into "needy" and "non-needy" are ignored. After all, as used in the literature the classification techniques do not discount chance errors of measurement when distinguishing a minority of under-privileged areas when areas differ along a continuum; the studies have to some extent, depended on them. The techniques are all too likely to select areas in which conditions are in fact better than some of those ignored. Moreover, as I argued from American evidence before this type of technique was applied to the selection of small areas in this country, there is evidence that problems are not highly concentrated in these areas (Davies, 1968; Hatch and Sherrott, 1973).

Our conclusions are clear. First, more elaborate techniques are required to establish and estimate the causal connections between need and demand, and to explore methods of "grounding" our need concepts better. Secondly, the survey has an important role to play in this work, but surveys should be used in conjunction with other collections of data. Thirdly, two principles should be applied, except where there are good reasons for not doing so: need indicators should be based on judgments that have been legitimized by the democratic political processes; and, since it is desirable to obtain the maximum information that data can properly yield, they should incorporate as strong a set of judgments as are compatible with legitimacy derived from these processes. Fourthly, need indicators, whether ratio scale indicators or making weaker assumptions about levels of measurement, should all be relative in the sense that they should take into account variations in the intensity of needs; that is, they should treat need as a variable rather than an attribute.

Service Provision and Local Needs

The work done on the measurement of needs has yielded some data of real utility to the professional and politician, although this work needs to be developed. I promised to discuss service provision as well as local needs. One could best relate needs and provision if one had indicators of service output. One has to search hard for any basis for computing indicators of attainment of the broad goals of the personal social services among the data now collected. The reasons are similar to those which make it difficult to measure outputs in other state services without product markets. The intellectual device of treating the activities as investment in human capital looks an implausible way of making it possible to measure the total value of all but a few personal social services, although, no doubt, it could be used to assess one component of this in at least some services. Because measurement tools and suitable collections of data do not exist, many of the achievements of the personal social services cannot at present be measured. It is difficult to see how the achievement of the personal social services catering for individuals and small groups can be measured without individualized data systems making full use of computers, since many measures of achievement amount to indicators of what social workers call movement in the units being helped. Some departments in this country have experimented with such systems, and a substantial number of American and Canadian agencies have done so. The difficulties are political, ethical and theoretical rather than technical.

Because we lack output indicators in the personal social services, we have to rely principally upon patterns of provision of input. However, we are by no means certain about what additional inputs could do most to increase outputs. The central government departments responsible for the personal social services had no doubts in their evidence to the Royal Commission on Local Government in England in 1967. The Ministry of Health wrote:

> The quality of these services . . . which are largely professional, depends primarily on the calibre of staff, both field workers and senior staff (Ministry of Health, 1967).

Similarly, the Home Office wrote that:

> inefficiency or indifferent performance, where they are met, can usually be attributed to personal factors (for instance, a poor children's officer, or poor coordination between chief officers of the relevant services) or to poor quality staff (The Home Office, 1967).

In oral evidence, a Home Office witness claimed that:

> The major factor (in causing a better or worse children's service) was the personality and quality of the chief officers and the staff. This is far too important for any other factor to become predominant (Royal Commission on Local Government in England, 1967).

This view, that the quality of staff is the major determinant of standards, has been put forward by other social workers, and seems to be held almost without qualification by social workers themselves. It has also been suggested that the continuity in the conditions that create a staff which is of high calibre allows differences in standards to consolidate and grow wider (The Home Office, 1967). But it has been shown that variations in indices of staff calibre are almost completely unrelated to patterns of provision of welfare services, and are not closely associated with most patterns of provision of children's services (Davies *et al.*, 1971, 1972). These studies measured staff calibre using indicators of qualifications and experience. It is possible that staff calibre is not associated with age and qualifications. Or perhaps the indicators of patterns are not associated with standards (though many of the indicators were chosen because they were expected to reflect standards). But it seems more plausible to infer that if, as one would expect, staff calibre is an important determinant of standards, it is an important determinant of some aspects only, and these are some of the most difficult to measure with existing data. It would be unreasonable to conclude, therefore, that the training of staff was of little importance in determining standards, although its consequence may have been exaggerated. A not unimportant reason why it is so essential to establish forms of data collection which will allow us to measure the attainment of goals is that we might then be able to build models and undertake other studies which would allow us to assess the contribution of skilled manpower better.

If the importance of the calibre of staff for variations in standards may have been exaggerated, the importance of the stock of physical capital of buildings and equipment may by some have been understated. There is evidence of various kinds to support the theory that many of the features of variations in patterns of provision of services are the consequence of the differing inheritances of physical (as well as human) capital; that, in the short run, at least, the stock of capital is not adjustable in response to demand, so that demand is deflected towards other components of the system, thus altering the roles of each service. For instance, county borough children's departments which had to cope with a heavy pressure of demand, but which did not have a compensating variation in the number of places in children's homes, tended to have a higher proportion of the children in foster homes— particularly foster homes outside the care authority's area; and of those boarded out outside the care authority's area, higher proportions tended to be supervised by the authority in that area rather than the authority whose legal responsibility it was. These authorities also tended to depend more on voluntary organization homes. Also the courts tended to commit higher proportions of children to approved school than to children's department care. It is not simply that the children's service systems whose area's capital stock was under pressure relied more on facilities provided by other areas; the roles of the services differed in other ways. The rate of turnover of children in homes was higher; the authorities claimed that the effect of preventive work in keeping children out of care was greater; more children were in temporary accommodation in relation to the number in children's department care; and more were in health department nurseries and education department nursery schools in relation to the number in children's department nurseries. The children's service was affected in other ways. For instance, the authorities tended to appoint inexperienced and semi-qualified officers as a response to the high pressure of demand. This is necessarily an over-simplification of complicated results; but the inference seems clear. The same was true of welfare departments. Although the supply of domiciliary services does not appear to affect the number of places in residential homes, the number of places appears to have an effect on the supply of domiciliary services. Given the pressure of demand, therefore, the system finds a way of adjusting other services to those which are in fixed supply in the short run. (Davies *et al.*, 1971; Davies *et al.*, 1972). Evidence that the services operate as systems, and that they respond to need (operating through demand) is new. Only three or four years ago, research had failed to discover it in one area where it is now clearest—the authority differences in patterns of provision having been attributed to the policies and preferences of decision-makers (Packman, 1969). The academic authority on the personal social services who wrote that:

> in the past, the quality, extent and nature of the personal social services have been largely supply determined . . . the actual level and pattern of need has played comparatively little part

reflected the state of understanding at that time. (Parker, 1970).

Although it is clear that the response to need (through demand) is systemic, there are clear signs that different dimensions of need call forth responses to different degrees and of different kinds. Constraints on supply help to cause this, but so may factors whose influences are more amenable to control. For example, capital investment in residential homes for the elderly is more sensitive to the demographic structure than to bad housing, poverty, and their correlates which have had a substantial effect on decision about the relative needs of individuals for a place in a home. This may be partly due to the Department of Health's loan sanction policy. Some model-building which takes into account that local authority allocations between broad departmental budget heads may be intermediate in causal priority between the characteristics of an area's population and its capital expenditure on homes, suggests that it is likely that the age structure of a population may have a stronger impact on expenditure on homes through its political impact on the broad strategic priorities of the council. A second example of different dimensions of need calling forth responses of different kinds is that bad social conditions—poor housing, low incomes and related characteristics—tend to be associated with a reliance in the mid-1960s on approved school rather than children's department care. There are several possible elements in an explanation of this: no doubt, the fact that higher proportions of children tended to enter care through the Courts reflected differences between the Court's and children's department's attitudes to treatment (although the Court's decisions are to some degree influenced by children's department policies). It also reflected the pressure on the scarcity of resources in children's departments, as well as the probability that delinquency is a more important symptom of child care problems in the areas and elsewhere and that both the Courts and the children's departments perceived that different treatment was appropriate.

If we are to assess the case for controlling what has been called the "degree of territorial justice"—the degree to which the standards of service provision and needs are correlated between areas—we must understand not only the operation of services as systems and the apparent responsiveness of their provision to needs, but also the influence of other factors on provision. Some things are clear. After thirty years of deficiency grants, the relative wealth of authorities does not itself have the pervasive influence on the pattern of local provision, although it may influence the provision of some services, (like domiciliary health services). In some ways, this makes problems of control more rather than less difficult. Financial subventions from the central government to local authorities for special purposes have to form part of a package whose purpose is to operate on local authorities' priorities—on their perception of those of their problems which are most important to tackle. The relatively poor authorities are not in the position that they were in during the 1920s and 1930s, unable to build tuberculosis sanatoria that they wanted because they could not raise the money to make use of the percentage central government grant then available. Local authorities, jealous of their autonomy and sensitive to political differences between themselves and the central government, never behaved like the economic men to the degree that many writing about the grant system have supposed. Certainly with few exceptions, evidence shows that the political balance at the local level has a considerable impact on the level of total expenditure in the authority, the Labour party being the spending party at local as well as national level. Moreover, through its effect on the total level of spending, it has a pervasive effect on the provision of resources throughout the authority, including an effect on the Council's broad spending priorities as these are reflected in the distribution of expenditure between departments. The party political balance also influences provision in less far-reaching ways: for instance, authorities with a high proportion of their seats controlled by the Labour party have children's service systems that are more independent of other forms of provision (probably thereby showing greater faith in municipal enterprise), and they have more generous charging policies for home helps.

Conclusion

The impression, therefore, with which one is left is of new needs being recognized of rapid development in the tools that must be used to map them, of deepening understanding of how services might be used to meet these needs, and of the behaviour of the political processes and organisations which influence the provision and effectiveness of the services.

Note

Professor Townsend raised some of the difficulties in one of his earliest works that attempted to measure "needs":

> Some people who plead for support may be quite capable of continuing to manage for themselves. Others who protest their independence may be in serious need of help. Indeed, it is sometimes difficult to decide what in fact their attitude is. People who are becoming infirm are often uncertain of the extent of their capacities and this uncertainty may be reflected in different opinions given on succeeding days, or even within the compass of a single interview. Another problem is that many people have only the haziest idea of what in fact a particular service consists of and, without giving some information, it is hard to expect them to come to a considered judgment. But this is a common problem—perhaps the basic problem in all social studies which attempts to gauge attitudes . . . Rules for the external determination of need have to be drawn very wide to begin to cover individual situations . . . if rational decisions about whether they need help are to be made then questions have to be asked not only about infirmity and the availability of help, but also income, housing, the nearness of particular kinds of shops, the frequency of a bus service, and so on. This can quickly become a complicated exercise. In a variety of ways the individual's condition and his circumstances have to be compared with the conditions and circumstances of other individuals in the same society (a) of like age and sex and (b) of a different generation. They also have to be compared with (c) the conditions and circumstances which were experienced by the individual at an earlier age. In sociological terms 'need' can only be revealed systematically by calling up the concepts of 'reference group' and referred experience

(Townsend and Wedderburn, 1965, pp. 44–45).

The sociologists of health have made some of the same points for perceptions of sickness. Professor Shanas specifically writes about the health perceptions of the elderly, and describes the self-assessment of health as "idiosyncratic":

> Self-assessment of health among the elderly, may be as closely related to subjective feeling states as to objective measures of incapacity

(Shanas *et al.*, 1968).

In the same study, Professor Shanas wrote that:

> The index of incapacity, although designed to measure functioning among old people, also may be an indicator of the use of medical care among the aged

(ibid., p. 35).

Dr. Malcolm Brown and his co-authors comment similarly about the lack of proper definitions of "chronic sickness" and "disability", describing them as "arbitrary and subjective"; they point out that figures from different surveys are not comparable which partly explains the 100 per cent difference in the proportion of households estimated to contain a chronic sick or disabled person in the Isle of Wight and the comparable estimate in Miss Harris's national survey in terms of the definitions adopted by the different populations (Brown *et al.*, 1972). Miss Sainsbury clearly describes some of the ways in which the assessment of handicaps is subject to error in Chapter 3 of *Registered as Disabled*. Miss Sainsbury re-classified the degree of handicap of some of her respondents because of clear bias in self-assessment (Sainsbury, 1970). When apparently exact indicators of such handicaps as partial-sightedness or indoor capacity are available, their relationship to the handicap that the impairment implies for leading a normal life is not clearly established. The inexactness of the Government Social Survey techniques of measuring handicap is evident in their discussions on pp. 2–16 of *Handicap and Impairment in Great Britain*, pp. 28–30 of *Sample Surveys in Local Authority Areas* (Harris *et al.*, 1971; Harris and Head, 1971).

References

Barker, P. and Harvey, J. (1969). Facing two ways: between the 60s and the 70s. *New. Soc.*, **18,** 847–50.

Bennett, A. and Garrard, J. (1971). A validated interview schedule for use in population surveys of chronic disease and disability. *Br. J. prev. soc. Med.*, **25,** 2.

Brown, M. J., Thomas, H. M., and Smith, A. (1972). *Survey of the Physically Handicapped in the Isle of Wight.* University of Birmingham.

Craig, J. and Driver, A. (1972). The identification and comparison of small areas of adverse social conditions. *J. R. statist. Soc.*, **C, 21,** 1.

Davies, B. (1968). *Social Needs and Resources in Local Services.* London: Michael Joseph.

Davies, B., Barton, A. J. and McMillan, I. (1971). *Variations in Services for the Aged.* London: Bell.

Davies, B., Barton, A. J., McMillan, I. and Williamson, K. (1972). *Variations in Children's Services among British Urban Authorities.* London: Bell.

Harris, A. (1960). *Meals on Wheels for Old People.* London: National Corporation for the Care of Old People.

Harris, A. (1968). *Social Welfare for the Elderly,* I and II. London: H.M.S.O.

Harris, A., Cox, C. and Smith, L. (1971). *Handicap and Impairment in Great Britain.* London: H.M.S.O.

Harris, A. and Head, E. (1971). *Sample Surveys in Local Authority Areas.* London: H.M.S.O.

Hatch, S. and Sherrott, R. (1973). Positive discrimination and the distribution of deprivations. *Policy and Politics*, **1,** 3.

Head, J. G. (1966). On merit goods. *Finanzarchiv.*, 1–29.

Hoinville, G. (1971). Evaluating community preferences. In *Cost Benefit Analysis.* Institute of Municipal Treasurers and Accountants.

Home Office. (1967). *Written Evidence of the Home Office to the Royal Commission on Local Government in England.* London: H.M.S.O.

Jefferys, M. (1971). A set of tests for measuring motor impairment in prevalence studies. *J. chron. Dis.*, **22,** 5.

Martin, I., Flynn, M., Flynn, P. and Mellor, N. (1972). The Liverpool social malaise study. *Social Trends*, **3.**

Ministry of Health. (1967). *Written Evidence of the Ministry of Health to the Royal Commission on Local Government in England.* London: H.M.S.O.

Musgrave, R. A. (1959). *The Theory of Public Finance.* New York: Wiley.

Packman, J. (1969). *Child Care: Needs and Numbers.* London: Allen and Unwin.

Parker, R. A. (1970). The future of the personal social services. *Polit. Quart.*, **51.**

Royal Commission on Local Government in England. (1967). *Minutes of Evidence,* **3,** question 241. London: H.M.S.O.

Sainsbury, S. (1970). *Registered as Disabled.* London: Bell.

Shanas, E., Townsend, P., Wedderburn, D., Milhog, P., Friss, H. and Stehouwer, J. (1968). *Old People in Three Industrial Societies.* London: Routledge and Kegan Paul.

Townsend, P. and Wedderburn, D. (1965). *The Aged in the Welfare State.* London: Bell.

The Future Need
for New Towns in Britain

DAVID HALL

Town and Country Planning Association, London, England

My brief for this chapter was a little more than my title implies. It was to define "the problems arising from the increasing need for new towns as the population grows and the economy develops". As the Director of an organization which has advocated the need for new towns for the last seventy years, I was much encouraged by the implied acceptance in that brief of the continuing need for new towns. It is not a case which is accepted by everyone although, nevertheless, it has been accepted by the three main political parties, with varying strengths of commitment, since the last war.

Although I do indeed intend to concentrate on the problems arising from this need, I think it is still worth spelling out the case itself and to do this I must first define what I mean by a "new town".

The idea of garden cities, as they were called, was first put forward by Ebenezer Howard in his book, *Garden Cities of Tomorrow—A Path Towards Peaceful Reform*. As a means of relieving the congestion and overcrowding of big cities he argued that people and jobs should be encouraged to move from them to new self-contained communities of limited size (30–50 thousand population), located beyond a green belt which would surround the old urban area and within which belt no further development would be allowed. Such self-contained communities would provide jobs near to people's homes, homes near to countryside, and enable the old urban areas to be redeveloped more spaciously. Two other very important and often overlooked aspects of Howard's idea were firstly, that he saw garden cities not only being

161

used to relieve urban congestion but also to provide growth points in declining areas, and secondly that although he set a size limit he foresaw that with the success of a particular garden city the pressures would be such as to make it exceed his optimum limit; he therefore proposed the ultimate development of sub-regional clusters, what he called social cities.

The early new towns started after the war were originally given target populations approximately in acordance with Howard's optimum size. Since then, however, there has been a substantial change in their scale and this is perhaps best demonstrated by the fact that twenty-three out of the twenty-eight new towns now designated in England, Wales and Scotland have target populations larger than Howard's limit, twelve of them with a hundred thousand population or more. These twenty-three new towns include several of the early new towns which have had their target populations increased once and sometimes twice.

Increasing the size of new towns is seen to have several advantages. It is found that they can attract industry more easily and can therefore be more selective; they can provide a larger number and variety of school-leavers which makes them particularly more attractive to office firms; the cost per head of basic services is less; a greater range of shops and other facilities can be provided and this is also more attractive to employers; and the larger the town the better use it is thought to make of scarce technical and administrative staffs.

A more fundamental evolution, however, than that of new towns becoming larger, is that we are beginning to see new towns based on existing towns of already substantial size. Of course, some of the early new towns were based on towns of a moderate size, the largest, Hemel Hempstead, had an original population of 21,000 when it was designated. But this is small compared with the four new towns designated in 1967 and 1968—Milton Keynes, Peterborough, Northampton, and Warrington. Milton Keynes, which is sometimes thought of as a "green field" new town nevertheless had an original population of 44,000 and it is to grow to a quarter of a million. Peterborough, however, had an original population of 83,000 and the other two well over a 100,000 population each. All of them are to grow to close on 200,000 or more.

Now these towns may very well not be regarded as "new" towns by the people who live in them, certainly not those who live in the older parts, but the fact is that they are new towns within the meaning of the Act. They are being developed under the New Towns' Act 1965 by development corporations of the same kind that started Harlow and

Stevenage and the other early new towns, and with an area embracing all the existing town and the land it is proposed to develop designated for acquisition by the development corporation if it needs it.

The main advantages, incidentally, that it was thought the expansion of *existing* towns in this way would have are: that the large existing population would tend to prevent age-imbalance of the kind experienced in earlier new towns; that people and employers would be more easily attracted where there was already an existing town centre and other facilities; and that those parts of these existing towns which were in need of redevelopment could be redeveloped to cope with a larger population and so be a more economic investment of public money.

The evolutionary story does not end there, however. The Central Lancashire New Town, designated in 1971, already has a population of a quarter of a million and includes the towns of Preston, Leyland and Chorley. It has a designated area of over 35,000 acres and is to grow to 430,000 by 1993. Thus here we see Howard's social city as more or less the basic concept from the start, for it is virtually certain that the Central Lancashire new town will be developed as a cluster of townships, both old and new.

Finally in this evolutionary process, we have the growth areas proposed in the Strategic Plan for the South East which was endorsed by the Government and accepted by the planning authorities in 1971. That plan foresaw the need to accommodate an additional four and a half million people in the south east of England outside Greater London by 1991, this being comprised of approximately one million people who will have moved out of Greater London itself (including their natural increase), and three and a half million being the natural increase of the rest of the region. A balance of inward and outward migration is expected. To accommodate this population the plan proposed that about two thirds of it should settle in five major and seven medium growth areas. The major growth areas would range in population size from half a million in the Crawley/Burgess Hill area to nearly one and a half million in the South Hampshire area for which the Structure Plan was published in September 1972. Between them these five major growth areas will accommodate close on two and a half million more people, roughly a doubling of their present aggregate populations. New *towns* is therefore hardly the word to describe them. Even new *cities*, in the traditional sense of the word, is not correct either, and it is too soon to describe them as new "social cities" though they must inevitably have many of the characteristics which Howard wanted for his subregional clusters. In the meantime, therefore, we are stuck with the rather mundane term, "growth area".

Although they may not be new towns of the kind we have seen so far, they will nevertheless substantially have the function that new towns have had in the south-east of England, that is to say they will act as locations for population and employment which moves out of Greater London. In addition, however, they will have two further functions: helping to accommodate the natural growth of the region and assisting in the redistribution of population and employment within it.

All this is not to say that the more traditional type of new town may not continue to be established, particularly in regions where the scale of growth is likely to be more moderate than in the south-east and yet where some new focus for it is required. The point is that, to put it crudely, new towns are now old hat but long live the social city.

Let me briefly put what I can call the statistical case for the range of new developments I have been describing. Many people with much wider demographic knowledge than I will know how notoriously variable are population forecasts. It is only a few years ago that we were being told to expect an increase of close on twenty million people in this country by the end of the century. Yet the latest population projection is for not much more than a third of that—seven million by the end of the century. On this experience it may even be foolish to assume any increase at all. Perhaps we shall soon reach a point of stability with births equalling deaths and a balance of inward and outward migration. However, I think I must assume that this point is unlikely to be reached within the next ten to twenty years and therefore a sizeable natural increase of the population will still have to be accommodated during that period.

It is much more certain that population will continue to move out of our existing built up areas and will also have to be accommodated. I have looked back only to 1939 but in every inter-censal period since then our major urban areas have lost population, to an increasing extent. Taking towns of a hundred thousand population or more, thirteen of them lost population in the 1939–51 period; eighteen of them lost population in the 1951–61 period and thirty (out of fifty-four) lost population in the 1961–71 period. There is no sign of this outward movement abating to any extent and indeed much of the evidence supports the view that it is likely to continue. The study of the *Long Term Population Distribution in Great Britain* published last year shows how the eight major cities of the country have densities very much higher than the average urban density for the country as a whole; when one couples this with the appalling conditions of overcrowding in which many of their inhabitants live, and recently described in the Shelter

Report, *Reprieve for Slums*, it is clear that people will continue to escape from these areas to more spacious conditions elsewhere, even if we were to begin a massive programme of environmental improvement in these areas straight away.

Given, therefore, the likely population increase and the movement out of our old urban areas by people escaping from overcrowded and sub-standard housing conditions, it is obvious that new housing must be provided with, of course, all the ancillary development. I would hope that it is equally obvious that most of this new accommodation should be provided in new towns/cities/growth areas or whatever you like to call them. There is no doubt that the development plan system operating since the war has prevented the worst excesses of urban sprawl that were seen in the inter-war period but it has not prevented a substantial amount of peripheral development taking place on the edge of existing towns whose internal structure could not absorb this growth. One can think of scores of examples of small and medium size towns whose populations have increased by fifty or a hundred per cent over a twenty year period and whose centres have therefore become congested with traffic and subjected to pressures for commercial development which has frequently destroyed their character. This is not so much because substantial peripheral development is always wrong but that the planning system itself has not provided the right sort of mechanism for ensuring that the consequential need for other development (more shopping space, car parks, an improved road system, schools, jobs etc.) can be satisfied in a properly phased and coordinated way.

This is why the powers of the New Towns Act are so important. A development corporation is empowered to buy all the land in the area it is developing, compulsorily if need be, and is responsible for much of the construction and all the coordination of the development in its area. Moreover, it is able to borrow substantial sums of money from the Government in order to finance the development. Thus, while the newness of a new town and some of its architectural style may not appeal to everyone, the fact is that, in general, housing, jobs, shops, schools, roads, open space etc. are all provided in balance. My case, therefore, is, perhaps, not so much for more new towns, but for more use of the New Towns Act. But what are the problems?

Firstly, there is the political problem. Use of the New Towns Act is a matter of central government intervention and a Conservative Government is not usually so enthusiastic about intervening in this way as a Labour one. Admittedly, the Government has announced recently that it is to use New Towns Act powers for the development of the urban growth arising from the development of the Third London Airport at Foulness. However, I have heard it said by a senior Government official that the Government is unlikely to make any further use of the New Towns Act in the south-east beyond that because of the outcry there would be from other regions in the country. This is not a convincing argument. My answer would simply be to use the New Towns Act more widely in the rest of the country but also where needed in the south-east.

Of course, substantial sums of central government funds are committed once it is decided to set up a New Town development corporation. About £900 million of Exchequer funds have been lent to New Town development corporations since the war. But it must be made clear that this is money which is *invested* by the Government. It is not profligate spending. The money is lent on 60 year loans and interest has to be paid on it each year together with repayment of part of the principal. Allowing for this, the fact is that the twelve earliest new towns last year showed a net aggregate profit of £2½ million. They did not, of course, show a profit in their early years because large capital sums had to be spent to acquire land, build roads, factories and houses, and start the town centres, before much revenue came in. Moreover, this profit is not what a private entrepreneur would consider adequate—but nor should it be. A private entrepreneur would not provide the same amount of open space, or landscaping or any subsidised housing. The difference between the profit that a private entrepreneur might have made (had he been willing to invest so much) and the profit actually made by the development corporation, represents the cost to the community at large of having decent environments in which people can live and work.

There is, of course, also the political problem at a more local level. In the early years of the new towns there was considerable objection from the local authorities where new towns were designated, sometimes because they did not want an influx of what they thought would be working class people and sometimes because they did not want a powerful new agency (the development corporation) operating in their midst and taking over what they thought should be their responsibilities. The fact is that these local authorities have changed their tune considerably since then as they have watched their rate incomes rocket.

Nevertheless, political opposition at the local level will undoubtedly be encountered if the New Towns Act is used to develop the substantial growth areas such as those proposed in the south-east. The choice therefore is either for the Government to ignore this local opposition (and possibly soften it by ensuring that the local authorities have a greater say in the deliberations of the development corporation), or to give the local authorities themselves powers similar to a New Town development corporation. This second possibility could have been realized in the new Local Government Act but unfortunately the Government had no stomach for it. The danger therefore is that the coordination of the development of these growth areas will be left to authorities without the powers to do it properly. In particular they will lack the same ability as New Town development corporations to assemble the land quickly and in large enough quantities; they will not have the same ability to borrow funds from the Government to acquire the land and carry out development; and they will not have the same ability to acquire the land at other than its full market value. Admittedly, there are ways in which the existing legislation could be bent or only amended slightly and which would enable local authorities to have these powers. But why bother when there is legislation already available which has stood the test of time—the New Towns Act.

It should perhaps be said that the Government is not unaware of these difficulties and in 1972 set up a working party, which reported later in the year, to examine some aspects of the problem, in particular the way in which local authorities might enter into partnership schemes with private enterprise for the carrying out of major developments in the growth areas in the south-east. Unfortunately, its recommendations seem to me to be of little value because its terms of reference limited it to consideration of schemes for the development of *residential* land only and not the integrated and related development of all other kinds.

One important reason for arguing that these growth areas should be developed by New Town types of agency is the one I have already touched on, that such an agency would be able to buy the land more cheaply than a local authority. A development corporation pays the market price of the land as it would be if no development corporation had been established, that is to say a price which excludes that part of the value of the land added by virtue of the development corporation's own activities. The principle behind this has always been that landowners should not be entitled to benefit from an increase in land values created as the result of a decision made for the general community advantage. This principle was, of course, behind the previous Government's legislation in setting up a Land Commission to collect a betterment levy. This has been a notoriously difficult principle to apply generally for all land but the one way in which the principle *has* worked is under the New Towns Act.

There is, however, a problem in applying this principle particularly to the growth areas in the south-east. This is that because it has been known for some time where these growth areas are and because they already contain a substantial amount of urban development, the fringes of which would in any case have a fairly high "hope" value, there may not be much difference between the price that any agency with development corporation powers might pay and the price which the land would fetch on the open market. I think this is a nettle that should be grasped largely by ignoring it. Although the "hope" value of land in these growth areas is certainly very high it is, I am sure, not as high as it will eventually be when it is known exactly what type of development is to take place on it and this increase in the value ought, in my opinion, to be recouped by the community through a public agency with development corporation-type powers. As a general principle I would say there is a strong case for adopting a similar system to the French "zones d'aménagement controllés" where at an appointed date before it is known specifically what development is to be allowed, land values are frozen for a specific period during which the detailed planning is worked out and the land acquired by a public agency. Space does not allow me to expand on this but I wish to say that I think it is fundamentally important for some system of this kind to be adopted, certainly in areas proposed for large scale development.

Turning to another problem which relates to my earlier point about the uncertainty of forecasting population increase, it will be very necessary for the plans for these growth areas to be flexible. They will need to be planned in such a way that they can operate as efficient urban units (or a collection of urban units) throughout their growth so that, if need be, their target populations can be reduced if it appears that population and/or employment growth in the region as a whole will not match up to what has been expected in the regional strategy. This will apply equally to other regions as well as the south-east. Moreover, as a part of the flexibility in the planning of the growth areas it will also be necessary for central government to be flexible in its issuing of Industrial Development Certificates and Office Development Permits. At present these are principally used to encourage new employment in development areas such as the north of England and South Wales, and to discourage it in growth regions such as the south east and the west Midlands. In my opinion the control exercised in the issuing of IDCs and ODPs will need to be relaxed in the growth areas proposed in regional plans. This will then act as an encouragement to employers to locate themsleves in the places where the regional plan wants them to go. All this control of employment will need to be carefully monitored in relation to the expectations of economic growth generally within a region and particularly in relation to how mobile it is.

Finally, there is the question of what physical form these large new urban concentrations should take. I referred earlier on to Howard's concept of the social city and we have yet to see this translated anywhere into actual development on the ground. Somehow one wants to provide the advantages of a wide choice of employment, recreational and educational opportunities which can only be economically viable in large urban areas with, on one hand, a choice of settlement size for people to live in and, on the other hand, without the disadvantages which have hitherto been associated with large urban concentrations. I am sure that the only way that this can be done will be to develop the concept of the sub-regional cluster with the units of the cluster varying in size and all readily accessible one to the other by good transport systems.

I would like finally to make a plea which may seem to cut across all that I have been saying. My brief was to discuss new towns and this I have done. But it should not be forgotten that one of the cardinal purposes of the new towns concept was not only to provide better living and working conditions for those people and employers who move to them but also to enable the old urban areas from which they have come to be replanned more spaciously. This, alas, has not been realized and, while I would not argue that there should be any diminution of the new towns programme nor dilution of policies for dispersal of population and employment (indeed these are still essential to the improvement of our old urban areas), we must now put considerably more public money into the redevelopment and rehabilitation of the inner parts of our large cities. The problems will be similar in kind, though on an even larger scale than those I have described for the new growth areas, but I am sure that the solutions lie in the same direction. Thus there is a case for using the development corporation-type of agency in our old urban areas and the London dockland area is an example of where this might first be tried. The agency would need to have similar land acquisition powers and the ability to buy that land using the same formula as development corporations do now. The political problems would be acute, but I think one can only remember that "faint heart ne'er won fair lady".

Competing Priorities
for Land Use

FRANCIS J. C. AMOS

City Planning Department, Liverpool, England

Introduction

A rapidly growing human population in a world of finite proportions inevitably poses the question of whether or not the world will continue to be able to support the growing numbers of humans. In recent years there has been increasing public discussion and consequently a greater public awareness of the different schools of thought on this issue.

The common factor even in the most extreme views is that, in response to shortages and pressures, the population (or certain parts of it) will adopt special courses of action based on priorities. It is the question of choice of priorities which now makes public discussion of population pressures of critical importance, for many of the choices will remain with individuals and even governmental choices can be made only with at least the tacit consent of the governed.

In Britain there are currently three major systems for the determination of priorities. The most simplistic and most widely acknowledged is the operation of the "natural forces of the market" which presumes that shortage generates demand, which improves profitability, which then generates production to correct the shortage. The second system is more complex and exists because of the shortcomings of the market system. It recognizes that shortages will not generate market demand either if potential consumers suffer from a gross overall shortage of resources or if the shortage cannot be expressed in monetary terms. Thus, on the basis of a social ethic, the market system is manipulated with a view to ensuring that all consumers can meet their essential needs. The third system should perhaps be regarded as a quality of the first two but its influence is so all-pervading that it merits a similar classification and status to the others. This third quality or system is the inertial characteristic of the set of institutions and practices which make up our social system and which constantly interact to reinforce each other and maintain the existing patterns of human activity.

The interplay between these systems of the market, of ethics and of stability and the way in which society resolves incompatibilities between them determines the priorities attached to all kinds of resource and activity. And, since nearly all activities require or affect the use of land it is worth looking at land use priorities in rather more detail.

Urban Expansion

One of the most common land issues and one of the best illustrations of the inter-play of policies, is the question of the rate at which agricultural land is developed for urban uses. In a strictly market system, since intensive urban uses are virtually bound to yield more profit per unit area than extensive agricultural uses, there could be an almost unrestricted growth of urban land uses. But there are series of priorities from the system of social ethics which operate to restrict this growth.

There is, for instance, a cultural myth that Britain is essentially a country of yeoman farmers. This now-a-days finds expression and strength in priorities related to international balances of payments and to the need to maintain the agricultural industry against the risk of war. There is also the belief, possibly stemming from the same origins, that large urban areas must, by definition, be unhealthy, and unpleasant, and should therefore be limited in size. Thirdly, there is the belief that the rural areas provide a landscape necessary for recreation and spiritual fulfilment.

As a consequence, this section of the market is manipulated by governmental powers to veto development proposals in certain areas, to subsidise agriculture in relation to crops and land quality and to subsidise high density urban development. To complement these measures local planning authorities are given additional powers to prescribe the limits of growth of individual settlements and to conserve rural areas.

The Issue of Ownership

The issue of the development of land is rendered even more complex, if one also takes into consideration the stabilizing effect of all those organizations which seek to at least maintain and, if possible, improve the position of their own particular interest. These extend from philanthropic amenity bodies to land owners who seek to derive environmental or financial benefit from the existing situation.

Indeed, ownership of land raises another series of issues in relation to priority. The public and legal attitude towards ownership is that an owner has a right to do what he likes with his land so long as it does not adversely affect the rights of other land owners or of the community in general and that he may only be deprived of ownership for the benefit of the community. This has meant that, while there are extensive controls to stop an owner doing what is thought to be undesirable there is very little to induce owners to do what is desirable. In fact, because of the unreality of trying to make an owner do what he does not want to do, government and local authorities have the power to compulsorily acquire a man's land so that, what needs to be done, can be done.

In conferring these powers of acquisition on central and local government it has been assumed that, if market conditions will not induce an owner to do what is needed, then it is the Government which must do it. In fact, the cultural attitudes to rights in property have ensured that the assumption shall be the practice, for it has prescribed that, in most cases, a public body may not convey to one private owner what it has compulsorily acquired from another. This has recently created a serious problem in relation to land for housing, for there has been a swing in the demand for new homes, away from local authority housing and towards private enterprise dwellings. Normal market operations have not made sufficient land available and public authorities have not been able to intervene. Here then is a conflict between the priority accorded to the rights of an owner in his land and the priority accorded to potential home owners.

Within the larger settlements and conurbations there are, in addition, other priorities which can further affect the way in which land is developed. One, in particular, is the demolition of slums. In many areas demolition presents opportunities to provide much needed open space and roads and new facilities for welfare, education and recreation. However, the priorities accorded to these improvements is lower than the priority for clearing slums and providing new dwellings with the result that land, earmarked for these purposes, lies unused within and around new residential development.

Industrial Imperatives

A further set of priorities which must be considered, both at the national and local scale, are those associated with industry and, since industry is largely dependent upon the market system the priorities are largely those of profitability. The mineral extraction industries call for a special mention in this respect for, collectively, they have probably done more damage to the environment in the name of profitability and national interest than any other group. Clearly location is determined by the geographical distribution of deposits but recent prospecting ventures in hitherto unworked and scenically attractive areas are now being energetically opposed on the grounds that the preservation areas of beauty should be of high priority.

While other types of industry share the same objective of profitability, their effect is somewhat different. As much manufacturing industry becomes increasingly more capital intensive and less labour intensive it tends to secure profitability by moving nearer to its major markets which, for the most part are the major concentrations of population. Thus there emerges a further conflict of priorities for profitability and for the social ethic of limiting the size of settlements. Even within these settlements there is yet another conflict, for new industrial processes often require large flat sites which can only be found on the agricultural margins of the urban area. Such sites not only extend the urban area by their own land requirements, but also by the housing and facilities needed for the people who work within them.

Individuals and Investment

It would, of course, be wrong to assume that, because this review has concentrated upon the activities and aspirations of large power blocks that the priorities of individuals are of no consequence. Indeed it is the cumulative effect of many individual desires for mobility which has generated massive land requirements for the motor car. While it is only necessary to listen to the demands of any motorist for road space coupled with his complaints about the quality of the environment, to reveal a host of conflicting priorities about the use of land.

Similarly, urban dwellers always pushing outward in search of a better environment which they destroy in their search are displaying conflicts of priority within the social ethical system itself.

For many individuals and organisations land is seen not so much as a resource but rather as an investment. Obviously at times when money values are depreciating and other forms of investment seem insecure, land can be an attractive alternative, especially in urban areas or potential urban areas where there is not only the prospect of a high rate of interest but also a substantial capital appreciation. It is this concept of land which has contributed to the recent escalation in land values and which generate pressures for any use of land which will enhance its value. Thus, the more common situation in which land acquires value because there is competition for its use is reversed so that land uses have been created solely to enhance the value of the land.

Reconciling Priorities

There are two philosophical views which may be adapted towards these competing priorities. One view is the passive acceptance that a balance will emerge only by allowing the law of the jungle to prevail and the most powerful, but not necessarily the most important, priorities to dominate. The other view is the more deterministic attitude that society should attempt to impose some order so that the most important priorities prevail.

The first view requires very little specific action on the part of society but the second immediately poses questions of how to identify the important priorities and how to accord them the power which they merit. The simplistic answer to these questions is that the making of these decisions is the art of government, but many would hold that such choices cannot be made purely on a subjective basis and that more scientific methods should be used.

In this respect, the investigation into the siting of the new London Airport may be regarded as a milestone in political decision making for two reasons. Firstly, because it was the first attempt to base a decision on the systematic examination of all the detectable relevant priorities. Secondly, because it revealed that a great deal has yet to be done before a reliable method of comparing qualitatively different phenomena is available.

The essential weakness of cost-benefit studies used for the airport and other studies is that they have to establish costs and benefits in terms of profitability and the social ethics referred to earlier in the paper. However, while profitability is specific and calculable, social ethics are heterogeneous, unspecific and incalculable. It could well be that this weakness will continue until some universal system or criteria of evaluation is identified. It is in this connection that the current debate about the rate of consumption of natural resources, is of particular relevance. In this debate even the most optimistic would accept that it would be prudent to husband natural resources, and the criteria of conservation and regeneration could possibly be the basis of universal evaluation of costs and benefits.

Such a system would, however, bring into question more than the competition between different types of land use. Indeed, the methods employed, particularly in so far as they consumed natural resources, could be a matter for more critical manipulation.

In Britain, because of our high population density and intensive economy the lessons of land use control have begun to be learnt but the lessons of resource control are still shunned and even when learnt will be more difficult to apply on a national basis.

The sophisticated high technology societies have within them practices which are far more damaging than the potlatch ceremonies of North America and the sacred cows of India. Society needs a more comprehensible and holistic method of ensuring that the most beneficial priorities prevail. Without it mankind could be committed to perpetual strife even if survivial is not threatened.

Index